# RECIPES FOR PEACE
# مطبخ السلام

---

Vegan cookbook
from the traditional Arab cuisine

كتاب وصفات خُضرية
من المطبخ العربي

---

Kifah Dasuki
كفاح دسوقي

KIFAHS

ISBN:1975891627
ISBN-13: 978-1975891626

*This book is my gift to you, because i want you to be the change in our world*

*with love*
*Kifah*

# Recipes For Peace
## Kifah Dasuki

**Hebrew Editor** Shiri Brook-Sagie | التحرير اللغوي بالعبريّة شيري بروك-ساجي
**Hebrew Copy-Editing** Yuval Kaplan | التدقيق بالعبريّة يوفال كابلان
**Arabic Translation** Ahad Dasuki | الترجمة للعربية عهد دسوقي
**Arabic Translation Editor** Asma Agbarieh-Zahalka | التحرير اللغوي بالعربيّة أسماء إغبارية-زحالقة
**Arabic Proofreader** Asma Agbarieh-Zahalka | التدقيق بالعربيّة أسماء إغبارية-زحالقة
**English Translation** Tom C. Atkins | الترجمة للانجليزية: توم اتكينس
**English Translation Editor** Lindsay Semel | التحرير اللغوي بالانجليزية ليندسي سيميل
**Book and Cover Design** Hadar Holleman - "Holle Studio" | تصميم الكتاب هدارهولمان
**Food Designer** Hila Cohen-Liron | تصميم غذاء هيلا كوهن-ليرون
**Photography** Shalev Man | تصوير شاليف مان

---

**Follow me**
**For my cooking page:** facebook.com/vegalush
**For my website:** www.kifahs.com
**Contact me at:** kifah@kifahs.com

Healthy food and less stress will make
you happier in your life  and they will
turn you to a  productive person and
successful one
Therefore, I have decided to send You
A FREE E-BOOK >> Scan QR
And guess what? you
can also receive a secret recipe just for
Recipes for Peace readers
all in on Scan

This E-book is about reducing stress
and amplifies meditation
I hope you will like it in addition to the
vegan cookbook you have purchased
and don't forget to make the Secret
Recipe and share it with me

# Introduction

## مــقــدمــة

My love for food came from my father, mother, and grandmother. People say that if you love to eat, you automatically can cook – and sure enough, I also learned my basic cooking skills from them.

As I watched my grandmother cooking our traditional dishes, the family's compliments swelling her with satisfaction and pride, a great passion for food was born in me. When I was older, I stood beside my mother in the kitchen, trying to mimic her cooking techniques. Sometimes I also helped my father, especially when he prepared his famous winter dish – fresh forest mushrooms with fried onion. Even though I only chopped the mushrooms, I felt the passion grow, fed by the delight of those who tasted the dish, as I came to know the same pride my grandmother felt. The passion only intensified with the years, and continues to motivate me today.

I became vegan after listening to a lecture that exposed me to the suffering that animals undergo on their way to our plate. I was shocked, and as a consumer of animal products, felt responsible and sorry for their pain. When I told my parents about my decision, they didn't protest as strongly as I'd expected, but they did make some jokes about their carnivorous daughter reversing a lifetime of habits in the blink of an eye. Today, I can say from the bottom of my heart, that this encounter with my parents gave me the will to commit to a vegan lifestyle.

After some years as a vegan, I decided to combine my two most fundamental beliefs – peace among people and peace between people and animals – into one project. The result is this book – Recipes For Peace.
Recipes For Peace is a collection of traditional Arab recipes, some originally vegan or vegetarian, and others that I've adapted for the vegan kitchen.

This is more than an ordinary cookbook, though. It was originally published in two languages – Hebrew and Arabic – side by side, written from a place of great love and with a real hope for change. A hope to fight fear and hostility and to nurture love and compassion. It all started when a friend suggested I write a book of all the recipes I'd published in various cooking forums. I liked the idea and decided to launch a crowdfunding campaign.

During that month-long campaign, I not only reached my fundraising goals, but also sold over a thousand copies of the book. Perhaps more importantly, though, that intensive month taught me how hungry society is for change. We want peace so badly, but don't know how to find it. The campaign's success showed me what a powerful force people can be. Working collectively, we really can change the status quo. We only need to create spaces in which we can realize our dreams, and to believe in them and in ourselves.

A Recipes For Peace is my message to you. I believe we can enjoy high-quality food without harming animals. We can take responsibility for the role we play in perpetuating the pain and abuse that the food industry causes to animals, and use our influence to reduce their suffering. A Recipes For Peace also represents my hope for a change in the relations between Jews and Arabs. For breaking down the walls of fear and frustration that divide us, for knowing each other, for communication, understanding, forgiveness, and for reaching out to each other for peace and love.

Last year, I organized a meeting of Jews and Arabs from all across the political and religious spectrums. We sat in Yarkon Park and discussed this and that beside a table heaped with delicacies. We all started as strangers, and as we spoke, we learned each other's life stories in a respectful, accepting way. The meeting strengthened my conviction that what makes us people is fundamentally the same. Perhaps we have different stories and agendas, but if we can see beyond our egos and fears, we can resolve our conflicts.

This book is divided into three chapters: "The Village," "Tel Aviv," and "Prague," according to the different phases of my life. As an Arab, I have always lived as a minority, first among a Jewish majority and then among a Czech one. Fear and frustration were therefore my lot, as was the hope for a better future. In each chapter, you will find a variety of dishes created in and inspired by that phase.
At the end of the book, you'll find dietary advice for the various dishes, and suggestions for healthy upgrades. Most of the ingredients can be found in supermarkets, and the rest in natural food stores. You can find more specialized products like vine leaves, bush okra, and frikeh in Arab villages and mixed cities in Israel or at your local Middle Eastern food stores. Ask the locals, come in, smile, and say Marhaba (hello), and I'm sure you'll find what you need.

I chose to use home measurements (such as a cup or a teaspoon), because the recipes are intended for home cooking. Only a few times have I specified a precise weight in grams, and even then it isn't necessary. All of the recipes have been tested by a group of cooking enthusiasts who prepared and tasted the dishes, shared their opinions, and gave critiques to help me improve when necessary. In your own kitchen, even if you approximate the quantities, I believe you'll be successful, especially as you play with the recipes time after time. The recipes start simple and become progressively more complex.

I hope and believe that A Recipes For Peace will enrich your daily cooking, family dinners, and festive meals. Who knows? Maybe the desire to read the recipes in Arabic or English will inspire you to learn a new language.
Cook, spread love and be the change!

Yours,
Kifah

# TABLE OF CONTENTS
## الفهرس

# Prague

براغ

## 110

# Basic Recipes

وصفات اساسيّة

## 158

# The Village
## القرية

### A Seed Sprouts
#### بُرعم ينمو

# Chapter one

# The Village

# القرية

My name, Kifah, means 'struggle.' Rest assured, it is not a violent struggle, but a mental one, a struggle to achieve life goals. I see my name as an obligation. It carries not only a calling but also a heavy responsibility. So far, I can say that it has faithfully represented my life.

I was born in the village of Fureidis, which in English means "paradise." I grew up on top of a mountain, with my window facing an open field. It really could be paradise, if only life were so simple...

I'm the eldest child of five – four girls and a boy. My family was warm and caring, but I wasn't an obedient child, so despite their great love, I often felt I was wearing my parents down. I didn't always play by the rules, and while they embraced me with their right hand, their left was always ready to slap me. Still, they were proud of me and my achievements, and they always made sure I knew it.

The atmosphere at the only school in my village fostered in me a drive to excel. I enjoyed chemistry and math in particular and was an excellent student. I have to attribute my ambition to the fact that I am a quadruple minority. I am a woman, an Arab, a Muslim, and I come from a rural village, which put me under a strain that forced me to develop a strong and resilient personality.

While I was studying in my village, I never could have imagined what life had in store for me. I always knew that I would carve my own path rather than follow the one set out for me. That I would hold my head high while I walked and let the sun touch my dreams. But I never could have anticipated that I would become a liberal, feminist, vegan. I would never have guessed that I would publish my first book before I was thirty, or that it wouldn't be a stirring novel or a book of soul-scorching poetry, but a cookbook of vegan recipes from the Arab cuisine.

During all of the three main phases of my life – in Fureidis, Tel Aviv, and Prague – my journey has been long, winding, and filled with obstacles. I've had many sleepless nights and tear-soaked pillows alongside moments of joy and laughter. I remember feeling so angry with the world, with Israel, with the Jews, and with my horrible luck to have been born in such a hellhole. I was angry for being an ethnic and religious minority, and even angrier for being a woman. I was angry with the security guards in malls and their humiliating searches.

However, I never gave myself over completely to the anger, and never took the easy way out. I always tried to stretch my boundaries and discover my own potential, despite the limitations and difficulties. It took me a long time to let go of all my fears and learn to trust my mother's lessons not to judge or generalize. If at first I resented that I wasn't born with a silver spoon in my mouth, but instead as an Arab searching for her identity, today I realize that it was this very circumstance that gave me such a mountain to scale. Now I'll have to find a new peak to climb.

For now, I leave you with the recipes that recall the scent of my childhood in the village and of my struggles there – a scent of Kifah.

# VEGAN MANSAF
# (RUZ BIL LABEN)
## FRIED MINCE OVER RICE WITH
## VEGAN YOGHURT

الأرز باللبن المنسف

"Vegan mansaf" might sound like an oxymoron, since this festive Jordanian dish famously contains animal products – yoghurt and minced meat. But I missed it so much I had to revise it to fit my new completely vegan kitchen.

# INGREDIENTS

(Serves 4-6)

RICE

1/3 cup thin soup noodles
1 tablespoon olive oil
2 cups long jasmine rice
4 cups vegetable stock
   (recipe on page 161)
1 teaspoon nutmeg
1 teaspoon salt
½ teaspoon pepper

VEGAN MINCE

1 tablespoon oil
¼ cup vegan mince, homemade
   (see recipe on page 160)
   or store-bought
¼ teaspoon red paprika
¼ teaspoon dry garlic powder
Salt and pepper

SERVING

¼ cup roasted pine nuts
   and almonds

# PREPARATION

FOR THE RICE

Heat the oil in a pot over a low flame and fry the noodles until brown.
Add the rice and vegetable stock and mix. Add the spices, cover the pot and cook over low heat for 15 minutes, until most of the liquids have been absorbed. When only some of the liquid remains turn the fire off, cover the pot with a clean towel and put the lid over the towel. Let the rice rest for at least 15 minutes.

FOR THE VEGAN MINCE

Heat the oil in a deep pan, and stir in the mince and spices until thoroughly heated. Adjust the seasoning to taste.

FOR SERVING

Serve the rice in a deep dish with the vegan mince on top. Garnish with roasted pine nuts and almonds. Best served with warm, homemade yoghurt.

# المقادير

(لـ 4-6 وجبات)

للأرز

⅓ كوب شعيرية
1 ملعقة كبيرة زيت نباتي
2 كوب أرز ياسمين طويل مغسول جيّدًا
4 كوب مرق خضار
(الوصفة صفحة 161)
1 ملعقة صغيرة جوزة الطيب
1 ملعقة صغيرة ملح
½ ملعقة صغيرة فلفل أسود

لخلطة بروتين الصويا

1 ملعقة كبيرة زيت نباتي
¼ كوب بروتين الصويا المطحون سواء من صنع بيتي
(الوصفة صفحة 160) أو جاهز بالنكهة الطبيعية
¼ ملعقة صغيرة ببريكا حلوة
¼ ملعقة صغيرة بودرة الثوم
ملح وفلفل حسب الرغبة

للتقديم

¼ كوب صنوبر ولوز محمص

# طريقة التحضير

الأرز

يُغسل الأرز جيّدًا بالماء حتى يصبح الماء نقيًا. تُقلى الشعيرية مع قليل من الزيت في قدر على نار هادئة حتى تصبح داكنة اللون. يُضاف إليها الأرز ومرق الخضار (بنسبة 2 كوب مرق لكل كوب أرز)، تُنثَر الهارات وتُخلَط جميع المكوّنات. تُغطَّى القدر جيدا وتُترك على نار هادئة لمدة 15 دقيقة، وقبل أن يتبخر الماء كليا نطفئ النار ونغطي القدر بفوطة نظيفة. يُترك الأرز جانبًا لمدة ربع ساعة على الأقل.

بروتين الصويا

يقلَّب بروتين الصويا بمقلاة مع الزيت والهارات لعدة دقائق.

التقديم

يُسكَب الأرز في وعاء عميق وتُضاف إليه طبقة من بروتين الصويا ويُزيَّن بالصنوبر واللوز المحمص.

**Best to serve with a warm yoghurt.** Mix 3 cups of vegan yoghurt (see recipe on page 162), ¼ cup hot water, juice from 1 lemon and a pinch of salt in a pot and bring to a boil. In a bowl, dissolve 1 tablespoon corn starch in ¼ cup hot water. Stir the corn starch mixture gradually into the yoghurt until thick.

SERVING SUGGESTION

من المحبذ تقديم الوجبة إلى جانب اللبن النباتي الساخن. تُخلط 3 أكواب من اللبن الخضري (الوصفة صفحة 162) في قدر مع ¼ كوب من الماء الساخن وعصير ليمونة واحدة ورشّة ملح. ويُحرّك باستمرار على نار متوسطة حتى يغلي. تُذوَّب جانبًا ملعقة كبيرة من النشاء في ربع كوب من الماء البارد. ويُضاف المزيج للبن مع الاستمرار بالتحريك. يجب أن يكون اللبن رخوًا وإذا جمد يمكن إضافة القليل من الماء.

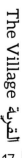

# MAQLUBA
## VEGGIE UPSIDE DOWN CAKE
المقلوبة

....................................................

The maqluba is one of the most splendid and iconic dishes of the Arab cuisine. Literally, it means "upside down," because it's a casserole of rice and vegetables served as an upside-down cake. When I started collecting recipes for this book, my father told me that my grandmother was the first woman to cook this dish in our village, Fureidis. I remember how the women in the village used to brag that they could cook maqluba, since they considered it a dish that requires experience, precision, and a fair amount of preparation in advance. Traditionally, it is cooked with pieces of chicken or meat, and served with cream or cooked yoghurt. For my recipe, I've made adjustments so you can enjoy a vegan version that is tasty, healthy and, I believe, more moral.

# INGREDIENTS

(Serves 4-6)

2 cups jasmine rice
2 small potatoes
2 small carrots
1 small eggplant
1 small cauliflower
1 tablespoon oil
4-5 cups vegetable stock
    (see recipe on page 161)
Salt and pepper
¼ teaspoon turmeric
¼ teaspoon ground nutmeg
¼ teaspoon cardamom (optional)

### SERVING

¼ cup roasted almonds

# PREPARATION

### FOR THE VEGETABLES

Preheat the oven to 180 degrees C (350 degrees F). Wash the rice well. Peel and slice the potatoes and carrot, keeping them separate from each other. Break the cauliflower into small pieces by hand. You can cut big pieces in half. Slice the eggplant, salt the slices and leave them on a paper towel for fifteen minutes. When the fluids have seeped out, blot the slices with a paper towel.

Arrange the vegetables on a baking dish lined with parchment paper, keeping each type of vegetable separate from the others. This will make it easier to arrange them in the pot later. Brush them with oil and roast for about 30 minutes, until partially soft.

### FOR THE MAQLUBA

Layer the roasted vegetables into a deep pot, sprinkling salt and pepper between each - first the potatoes, then the eggplant, the carrots and finally the cauliflower.

Pour the rice over the vegetables, then add in the vegetable stock and the spices. I recommend starting with 4 cups of liquid and adding more if needed – the liquid should be 1 cm (2/5 inch) above the rice. Using a long wooden spoon, carefully ventilate the rice by making 3-4 holes from the top of the rice to the bottom of the pan. This will allow the rice to cook thoroughly and the spices to reach all the layers. Cook over a medium heat for 30-40 minutes. You can add a cup of boiling water as the rice cooks – the liquids should stay 1 cm above the rice until the cooking is done. Let the casserole rest for at least 30 minutes before serving.

### FOR SERVING

Put a large tray over the pot, and carefully turn the pot upside down. If the maqluba doesn't come out whole, like a cake, no matter – you can use my secret: rearrange the vegetable layers in the bottom of a deep bowl. Cover with the rice, gently compress using a large spoon, and turn over again. This time, the maqluba should come out whole. If not, don't be disappointed – authentic Arab food is always messy! Maqluba is best served with a side of green salad or cold yoghurt (see recipe on page 162)

## المقادير

(لـ 4-6 وجبات)

2 كوب أرز الياسمين

2 حبة بطاطا صغيرة

2 حبة جزر صغيرة

1 حبة باذنجان صغيرة

1 رأس قرنبيط صغير

1 ملعقة كبيرة زيت

4-5 كوب مرق خضار
(الوصفة صفحة 161)

ملح وفلفل أسود حسب الرغبة

¼ ملعقة صغيرة كركم

¼ ملعقة صغيرة بهار جوزة الطيب

¼ ملعقة صغيرة هيل مطحون
(غير إلزامي)

### التقديم

¼ كوب لوز محمص

## طريقة التحضير

### الأرز

يُغسل الأرز جيّدًا.

### الخضار

تُقشّر جميع الخضار وتُقطّع إلى شرائح دائرية. إذا كانت زهور القرنبيط كبيرة، يمكن تقطيعها إلى أنصاف. تُوضع شرائح الباذنجان في صينية أو صحن كبير ويُرشّ عليها الملح وتُترك لمدة ربع ساعة حتى تفرز سوائلها، ثم تُجفّف جيّدًا بورق المطبخ.

تُرتّب الخضار كل نوع على حدة في صينية مغطاة بورق الخبز، وذلك ليسهل ترتيبها لاحقًا في القدر. يُضاف القليل من الزيت على الخضار وتُدخل إلى فرن مسخن مسبقا على حرارة 180 درجة وتُخبَز لمدة نصف ساعة حتى تشرف على النضج.

### طريقة الترتيب بالقدر

تُرتّب الخضار في قدر عميقة على شكل طبقات، ويُنثَر على كل طبقة الملح والفلفل الأسود. تُرتَّب طبقة البطاطا ثم الباذنجان وبعدها الجزر وأخيرًا الزهرة.

يُضاف الأرز فوق الخضار ثم تُسكَب 4 أكواب من مرق الخضار. وأخيرا تُضاف جميع البهارات.

بواسطة ملعقة خشبية طويلة نحفر حفرًا صغيرة داخل الأرز والخضار حتى تصل السوائل والبهارات إلى جميع الطبقات لينضج الأرز والخضار جيّدًا. تُوضع القدر على نار متوسطة وتُترَك لمدة 30-40 دقيقة. يمكن إضافة كوب من الماء المغلي أثناء الطهي إذا جفّ الماء قبل أن ينضج الأرز. من المهم جدًّا التأكد من ألّا يجفّ الماء تمامًا.

بعد انتهاء الطهي تُوضَع القدر جانبًا ليرتاح الأرز، لمدة نصف ساعة على الأقل.

### التقديم

تُوضَع على القدر صينية دائرية (أكبر من القدر) ثمّ تُقلَب القدر بحذر شديد للحصول على مقلوبة دائرية مثل شكل الكعكة. إذا لم تحصلوا على نتيجة مُرضية، يمكنكم اتّباع طريقتي: نرتب في وعاء عميق أصغر حجما من القدر، جميع محتويات القدر (نبدأ بالخضار) ونضغط عليها برفق بواسطة ملعقة كبيرة، ثم نقلب الوعاء مرة أخرى. هذه المرة ستنجحون في الحصول على الشكل المرغوب. وإذا لم يتمّ لكم ذلك، فلا بأس، المقلوبة غير المهندسة ألذّ طعمًا!

تُقدَّم المقلوبة مع سلطة الخضار أو اللبن المطبوخ (الوصفة صفحة 140).

# MAHASHI
## COLORFUL STUFFED VEGETABLE CASSEROLE

المحاشي

A fun, flavorful dish made of vegetables stuffed with rice and almonds and cooked in an aromatic spearmint and oregano vegetable stock. Using fresh, multicolored vegetables will make for a beautiful, juicy casserole.

# INGREDIENTS

(Serves 4)

## STUFFED VEGETABLES

3 bell peppers of different colors
1 small eggplant, preferably round
2 small zucchinis

## STUFFING

2 cups washed jasmine rice
1 small potato, diced
1 tablespoon dried oregano
1 tablespoon dried spearmint
½ cup crushed almonds
Salt and pepper

## STOCK

750 ml (about 3.2 cups) vegetable stock
    (see recipe on page 161)
4 tablespoon tomato paste
Salt and pepper
1 clove garlic

# PREPARATION

## FOR THE VEGETABLES

Take the tops off the bell peppers and keep them. Clean the seeds from the insides. Slice off the tops of the eggplant and zucchinis. If they won't stand on their own, you can flatten the bottoms by shaving a little bit away with a knife. Using a teaspoon, remove the centers and seeds, making sure to leave 1cm (2/5 inch) of flesh, so that the remaining hollow vegetables look like cups.

## FOR THE STUFFING

In a bowl, combine all of the stuffing ingredients. Gently fill the vegetables ¾ of the way (the rice expands during cooking). Put the tops back on the peppers.In a wide, deep pot combine all of the ingredients for the stock. Then gently place the stuffed vegetables into the mixture. The vegetables should be covered by the liquid. If necessary, add more liquid. Cook over a medium flame for 30-45 minutes, until the vegetables are soft and the rice is cooked. Take care not to overcook, so the vegetables have a firm texture and don't fall apart.

# المقادير

(لـ 4 وجبات)

## الخضار

3 حبات فلفل حلو بألوان مختلفة
1 حبة صغيرة باذنجان , مفضل مكوّر الشكل
2 حبة صغيرة كوسا

## للحشوة

2 كوب أرز ياسمين مغسول
1 حبة صغيرة بطاطا مقطّعة لمكعبات
1 ملعقة صغيرة اوريجانو
1 ملعقة صغيرة نعنع جاف
½ كوب لوز مطحون خشن
ملح وفلفل أسود حسب الرغبة

## لصلصة البندورة

750 مليلتر مرق خضار (الوصفة صفحة 161)
4 ملعقة كبيرة معجون البندورة
ملح وفلفل أسود حسب الرغبة
1 فص ثوم

# طريقة التحضير

## الخضار

يُقطع القسم العلوي من الفلفل وتُزال البذور. تُحفَر الكوسا والباذنجان وتُنظَّف جيّدًا.

## الحشوة

تُخلَط كل مكوّنات الحشوة في وعاء، وتُحشى بها حبات الخضار حتى ثلاثة أرباع حجمها، مع الأخذ بالاعتبار أن الأرز ينتفخ خلال الطهي. توضَع المحاشي بالترتيب في قدر كبيرة وعميقة. تُخلَط كل مكوّنات صلصلة البندورة وتُسكب فوق الخضار. تُترك القدر على نار متوسطة لمدة 30-45 دقيقة حتى تنضج. راعوا عدم الطهي أكثر من اللزوم كيلا تتفتّت المحاشي.

## التقديم

تُرتب المحاشي بالطبق وتُقدّم مع صلصة البندورة من قدر المحاشي.

Serve with cold, sour yoghurt (see recipe on page 162) or with the leftover stock.

SERVING SUGGESTION

يمكن تقديم اللبن البارد ( الوصفة صفحة 162) بالاضافة لصلصة البندورة.

# INGREDIENTS

(Serves 4-6)

1 medium sized cabbage

STUFFING

1 cups jasmine rice, washed
1 teaspoon nutmeg
1 teaspoon white pepper
½ teaspoon black pepper
Salt
¼ cup crushed cashews

COOKING

3-4 cups vegetable stock
(see recipe on page 161)
9-10 peeled garlic cloves
Juice from one big lemon (or more to taste)
Salt

# PREPARATION

Make a hole at the bottom of the cabbage by cutting around and removing the stem. Boil the cabbage in a deep, large pot for 30 minutes, until soft. Carefully remove the cabbage from the water, let it cool and separate the leaves gently, so they don't break. In batches of four, return the leaves to the pot for 2 more minutes over low heat. Let the leaves cool.

FOR THE STUFFING

Mix the (uncooked) rice with the spices in a bowl. Then add the cashews.
Slit every leaf along the middle, and cut out the stem. Put some rice at the far end of each leaf and roll. Prepare all the leaves in the same manner.

FOR COOKING

Empty the water you used to cook the cabbage leaves from the pot and arrange the stuffed leaves inside in rows. Between each layer put 3-4 whole garlic cloves.
Pour the vegetable stock over the stuffed leaves, making sure all the leaves are completely covered. Add lemon juice and salt to taste. Cover the pot, bring to a boil and cook over medium-low heat for 30-40 minutes, until the liquids have been absorbed. Serve with sour vegan yoghurt (see recipe on page 162).

المقاديــر

(لـ 4-6 وجبات)

1 ملفوف متوسط الحجم

الحشوة

1½ كوب أرز الياسمين (منقوع ومغسول)
1 ملعقة صغيرة بهار جوزة الطيب
1 ملعقة صغيرة فلفل أبيض
½ ملعقة صغيرة فلفل أسود
ملح حسب الرغبة
¼ كوب كاجو مطحون خشن

الصلصة

3-4 كوب مرق خضار (الوصفة صفحة 161)
9-10 فصوص ثوم مقشّر
عصير ليمونة واحدة
ملح حسب الرغبة

طريقة التحضير

الملفوف

يُسلَق الملفوف بعد نزع رأسه الصلب في قدر من الماء المغلي لمدة نصف ساعة. يُصفّى الملفوف ثم تُفصَّل أوراقه عنه بحذر، وتُسلَق كل أربع أو خمسة أوراق على حدة لمدة دقيقتين حتى تصبح طرية وتوضع جانبا حتى تبرد.

الخلطة

يُخلَط الأرز مع البهارات والكاجو. يُنزَع القسم الصلب من أوراق الملفوف، وتُحشى بالأرز وتُلفّ.

الطبخ

يُرتب الملفوف المحشي في القدر. تُوزَّع فصوص الثوم بين أوراق الملفوف وتُخلَط باقي مكوّنات الصلصة وتُسكَب في القدر. يُطهى الملفوف على نار متوسطة لمدة 30-40 دقيقة حتى ينضج.

يُرتب

يُقدّم مع اللبن الخضري البارد (الوصفة صفحة 162).

# MALFOUF STUFFED CABBAGE

## الملفوف المحشي

The name "malfouf" comes from the Arabic word for "wrapped," because of the way the cabbage leaves are wrapped around each other. Once you've perfected this dish and added just the right amounts of garlic and lemon, the result is addictive.

# MAJADARA WO SALATET AL-FIJEL
## RICE WITH LENTILS AND RADISH SALAD

المجـدرة وسلـطة الفجل

Rich, nutritious majadara, rice and lentils, is a staple of both Arab cuisine and vegan cuisine alike. There are several ways to prepare majadara. Variations might differ in the amount of rice (which traditionally was bulgur), the type of lentils, the amount of onion and the mode of cooking. Here is the recipe I like best to prepare – and to eat.

# INGREDIENTS

(Serves 4)

## MAJADARA

½ cup jasmine rice, washed
1 medium sized onion,
    cut into half-slices
1 cup green lentils, washed
4 cups vegetable stock
    (see recipe on page 161)
Salt and pepper

## RADISH SALAD

5 small radishes
Juice from ½ large lemon
1 tablespoon olive oil
Salt

# PREPARATION

## FOR THE MAJADARA

In a small-medium pot, fry the onion until brown
(two more minutes after golden). Add the lentils
and three cups of the stock, bring to a boil,
cover the pot and cook over medium heat for 25-
30 minutes, until the lentils are completely soft.
Add the rice and the remaining cup of stock.
Season with salt and pepper, and keep the
pot covered over medium heat for 10-15 more
minutes, until the rice is cooked. Turn the heat
off and let the pot rest, covered with a clean
towel, for 20 minutes.

## FOR THE RADISH SALAD

Grate the radishes. Add lemon juice, olive oil and
a pinch of salt and mix. Serve with the majadara.

---

The majadara can alternatively be served with a quick yoghurt salad:
In a bowl, mix diced cucumber, some chopped spearmint, ½ teaspoon
of salt and a crushed garlic clove. Dress with a cup of cold, sour yoghurt
(see recipe on page 162) mixed with a tablespoon of water.

BONUS
RECIPE

---

# المقادير

(لـ 4 وجبات)

## للمجدرة

½ كوب أرز الياسمين
1 بصلة متوسّطة الحجم ومقطّعة
لأنصاف دوائر
1 كوب عدس صحيح مغسول
4 كوب مرق خضار مغلي
(الوصفة صفحة 161)
ملح وفلفل أسود حسب الرغبة

## لسلطة الفجل

5 رؤوس فجل صغير
عصير نصف ليمونة
1 ملعقة كبيرة زيت زيتون
ملح حسب الرغبة

# طريقة التحضير

## المجدرة

يُقلى البصل جيّدًا في قدر صغيرة حتى يحمرّ (أنصح بالاستمرار بالقلي
دقيقتين بعد الاحمرار). يُضاف العدس و 3 أكواب من مرق الخُضار.
بعد أن تغلي جميع المكوّنات تُخفَّف الحرارة وتُترَك على نار متوسطة
حوالي 25-30 دقيقة حتى تنضج.
يُغسَل الأرز جيّدًا ويُضاف إلى القدر مع الكوب المتبقي من مرق
الخضار. يُنثَر الملح والفلفل الأسود وتُحرَّك المحتويات جميعها، وتُترَك
على النار لمدة 10-15 دقيقة أخرى. تُطفأ النار وتُغطَّى القدر بفوطة
نظيفة وتُترَك جانبًا لمدة 20 دقيقة.

## لسلطة الفجل

تُبرَش حبات الفجل بالمبرشة، ويُضاف إليها عصير الليمون وزيت
الزيتون ورشّة ملح، وتُقدّم مع المجدرة.

---

للتنويع. يمكن تقديم المجدرة مع سلطة الخيار باللبن الخضري :
تُقطّع حبة خيار خضراء لمكعبات صغيرة وتُخلط مع القليل من النعنع المفروم. نصف
ملعقة ملح. فص ثوم مفروم. كوب من اللبن النباتي (الوصفة صفحة 162)
وملعقة كبيرة من الماء البارد.

# MALUKHIYAH STEW WITH BLACK QUINOA

الملوخية والكينوا السوداء

The traditional malukhiyah is a rich stew made from the leaves of bush okra. The name is derived from the Arabic word for "king," because though it was cheap, it was considered fit to serve to kings. The dish originated and is most famous in Egyptian cuisine, but is also very widespread across the Arab world. I remember my mother's wonderful malukhiyah, which I ate eagerly as a child, with a lot of warm pita-bread and lemon. When I grew up, I tried to develop a vegan version of the beloved flavors. Ever since I developed this easy version, made simply from leaves, I won't give it up. The secret to a good vegan malukhiyah is using vegetable stock instead of water. It's best when cooked fresh and in season (summer). You can pick – or buy – a stock of fresh malukhiyah in season, and dry it in advance for the cold months' soups.

# INGREDIENTS

(Serves 4-6)

MALUKHIYAH

2 cups chopped malukhiyah, fresh or dry
4 cups vegetable stock (see recipe in page 161)
4-6 garlic cloves, cut in half
Salt

QUINOA

2 cups of black quinoa
4-5 cups of boiling vegetable
stock or water
Salt and pepper

# PREPARATION

FOR THE MALUKHIYAH

Wash the leaves well. Separate the leaves from
the stems and dry well. Chop using a sharp knife
(I don't advise using a food processor).
Heat the vegetable stock in a wide pan and add
the garlic and salt. Add the leaves only when the
water begins to boil, and stir well. Cover the pot
and cook over low heat for 10 more minutes.

FOR THE QUINOA

Wash the quinoa well under the tap until the
water runs clear. Strain well.
Bring the stock (or water) to boil in a pot, add the
quinoa, season with salt and pepper, cover the
pot and cook for 20 minutes over low heat. If the
liquids have been absorbed and the quinoa still
isn't cooked, add ½ a cup of boiling liquid and
cook until dry. Open the pot, cover it with a clean
towel, replace the lid and let the quinoa rest for
15 minutes.
To serve pour the malukhiyah over the quinoa in
a deep plate and eat with a lot of lemon.

## المقادير

(لـ 4-6 وجبات)

الملوخية

2 كوب ملوخية مفرومة طازجة
أو مجففة
4 كوب مرق خضار
(الوصفة صفحة 161)
4-6 فصوص ثوم مقطعة لأنصاف
ملح حسب الرغبة

الكينوا

2 كوب بذور كينوا سوداء
4-5 كوب ماء مغلي أو مرق خضار
ملح وفلفل أسود حسب الرغبة

## طريقة التحضير

الملوخية

تُغسل أوراق الملوخية بالماء وتُفرد على قطعة قماش حتى تجفّ، ثم تُفرَم فرمًا ناعمًا جدًّا.
يُغلى مرق الخضار في قدر مع الثوم، وتُضاف إليه الملوخية بالتدريج مع التحريك المستمر، حتى الحصول على قوام متجانس غير جامد ولا رخو. يُنثَر الملح وتُترك القدر لتغلي على نار هادئة لمدة 10 دقائق.

الكينوا

تُغسل حبوب الكينوا جيدا للتّخلص من مراراتها، تُوضع في قدر من الماء المغلي أو مرق الخضار ويُنثَر عليها الملح والفلفل الأسود. تُخفّف الحرارة وتُغطّى القدر وتُترك على نار هادئة. إذا تبخّرت السوائل دون أن تنضج الكينوا، يُضاف ربع كوب من الماء المغلي أو المرق وتُحرّك الكينوا جيّدًا، ثم تُغطّى وتُترك حتى تنضج.
يُرفَع الغطاء عن القدر وتُغطّى بفوطة مطبخ نظيفة ثم يُعاد الغطاء، وتُترَك لمدة ربع ساعة.
في طبق تقديم عميق تُوضَع الكينوا وتُسكَب فوقها الملوخية. تُؤكَّل بشهية بعد إضافة عصير الليمون.

# STEWED TOMATO OKRA | البامية

Okra is easy to prepare, tasty and nutritious. It's best to buy fresh okra in season rather than using frozen, but if you cook large quantities of this recipe while the okra's fresh, you can freeze portions for later. The secret to the success of the dish is in the precise cooking time and handling of the okra. To keep the okra from getting sticky and gooey, it's important not to overcook it, and to stir gently, to keep the pods intact.

## INGREDIENTS

(Serves 6)

1 kg (2 pounds) of green okra,
   fresh or frozen
1 large onion, chopped
4 garlic cloves, sliced
1 kg (2 pounds) ripe tomatoes
2 tablespoon tomato paste
¼ cup olive oil
Salt and pepper
½ sliced chili pepper (optional)

## المقادير

(لـ 6 وجبات)

1 كيلوغرام بامية طازجة او مُثلّجة
1 بصلة كبيرة الحجم مفرومة
4 فصوص ثوم مقطعة
1 كيلوغرام بندورة حمراء ناضجة
2 ملعقة كبيرة معجون البندورة
¼ كوب زيت زيتون
ملح وفلفل أسود حسب الرغبة
½ قرن فلفل حار مقطّع
(غير إلزامي)

## PREPARATION

Cut the stems off the okra pods leaving just enough so that the head of the pod remains intact. Wash and dry well.
In a wide pot, heat the olive oil and cook the onion until golden. Add the garlic and fry slightly. Add the okra and fry for 5-7 more minutes over medium heat. Gently stir while cooking. Dice three tomatoes and puree the rest in a food processor until smooth. Add the pureed tomatoes, diced tomatoes and tomato paste to the pot and stir gently.
Season with salt and pepper, cover the pot and cook for 20-25 more minutes over medium heat. While cooking, stir very carefully so the okra remains intact and doesn't turn sticky or gooey. Serve with white rice and garnish with green chili pepper.

## طريقة التحضير

تُقمَّع البامية وتُغسل وتُترك لتجفّ. يُقلَى البصل والثوم في قدر مع زيت الزيتون، ثم تُضاف البامية وتُقلَّب بعناية لمدة 5-7 دقائق. تُهرَس حبات البندورة أو تُفرَم في الخلاط ما عدا ثلاث حبات تُقطَّع إلى مكعبات. تُضاف البندورة المهروسة والمقطّعة ومعجون البندورة إلى القدر، ويُنثَر القليل من الملح والفلفل الأسود. تطهى البامية على نار هادئة لمدة 25 دقيقة مع مواصلة التحريك بحذر للحفاظ على حبات البامية كاملة. تُقدَّم مع الأرز الأبيض وتزيّن بالفلفل الحار.

# VEGAN BULGUR KUBEH | الكبة

Do I really need to mention that this is vegan kubeh? The whole book is, after all, completely vegan! But kubeh was the first traditional food I veganized. I can still remember how curious my father was to taste it, and how at first he refused to admit that my vegan kubeh was just as good as the original. It was the way he wolfed down the entire plate that gave him away. Sometimes actions speak louder than words. While this dish requires skill and a lot of patience (my mother's secret is to rinse her hands in cold water before rolling each kubbeh), when you see the expressions on your guests' faces, you'll forget everything you thought you knew about vegan food – and so will they!

# INGREDIENTS

(Makes 10 units)

CRUST

2 cups bulgur wheat
3 tablespoon flour
1 tablespoon sweet paprika
1 teaspoon salt

STUFFING

1 tablespoon olive oil
1 large onion, diced
1 cup vegan mince, homemade
  (see recipe on page 160) or store-bought
Salt and pepper
1 teaspoon sweet paprika
¼ teaspoon spicy paprika
¼ teaspoon white pepper
¼ teaspoon cinnamon
¼ cup pine nuts, roasted
1 liter (quart) deep-frying oil

# PREPARATION

## FOR THE CRUST

Put the bulgur in a large pot and soak in 4 cups warm water (pre-boiled in a kettle) for fifteen minutes, until the water is absorbed.
Move the bulgur to a bowl, add the flour and mix well. Blend the mixture in a food processor (small ones may require splitting the mixture to several batches) until you have a dough you can easily manage, not too dry and not too sticky. If it is too sticky, add a tablespoon of flour. Add the sweet paprika and knead well until you have a uniform, reddish dough. Let the dough rest for 15 minutes.

## FOR THE STUFFING

Heat the olive oil in a pan and fry the onion over medium heat until brown. Add the vegan mince. Mix well and fry for two more minutes.
Add all the spices and mix. Remove from the heat and let the mixture rest for 2 minutes. Add the roasted pine nuts. Stir well and cool well.

## FOR THE ASSEMBLING

Rinse your hands in cold water. Take a small ball of dough and, using your thumb, make a small dent in the middle. Twist your thumb slowly to make place for the stuffing. You'll know the space is the right size when the crust around it is 2 cm (4/5 inch) thick. Using a teaspoon, add some of the stuffing, close the ball over it and shape it into a kubeh. Make sure the crust isn't cracked and that the stuffing is compacted. In the same manner, prepare all of the kubehs.
In a large pot heat the deep-frying oil (make sure the oil is boiling, to keep the kubehs from breaking up) fry the kubehs for 2-3 minutes, until brown. Using a slotted spoon, take the kubehs out of the oil and onto a plate covered with a paper towel. Serve hot with tahini.

## FOR A HEALTHIER VERSION

Bake the kubeh in an oven preheated to 180 degrees C (350 degrees F) for 10 minutes, until brown. Keep in mind – the texture won't be as crunchy as when fried.

## المقادير
(لـ 10 أقراص)

**لعجينة الكبة**

- 2 كوب برغل
- 3 ملعقة كبيرة طحين
- 1 ملعقة كبيرة ببريكا حلوة
- 1 ملعقة صغيرة ملح

**للحشوة**

- 1 ملعقة كبيرة زيت زيتون
- 1 بصلة كبيرة مقطّعة لمكعبات
- 1 كوب بروتين الصويا المطحون سواء من صنع بيتي (الوصفة صفحة 160) أو جاهز بالنكهة الطبيعية
- ملح وفلفل أسود حسب الرغبة
- 1 ملعقة صغيرة ببريكا حلوة
- ¼ ملعقة صغيرة ببريكا حارّة
- ¼ ملعقة صغيرة فلفل أبيض
- ¼ ملعقة صغيرة قرفة مطحونة
- ¼ كوب صنوبر محمص
- 1 لتر زيت للقلي

## طريقة التحضير

### العجينة

يُنقَع البرغل مع أربعة أكواب من الماء المغلي لمدة ربع ساعة حتى يمتصّ الماء. يُضاف الطحين ويُخلَط جيّدًا ثم تُطحَن المكونات في الخلاط الكهربائي (يمكن تقسيم الكميات إذا كان الخلاط صغير الحجم). نعجن الكبة باليدين حتى نحصل على قوام متجانس ومتماسك. إذا كانت العجينة دبقة يمكن إضافة ملعقة طحين. تُضاف للعجينة ملعقة ببريكا وتُعجن جيّدًا، ثم تُغلَّف بالنايلون وتُترَك جانبًا لترتاح لمدة ربع ساعة.

### الحشوة

يُقلى البصل بالزيت على نار متوسطة حتى يصبح ذهبيّ اللون. يُضاف بروتين الصويا ويُحرّك جيّدًا، ثمّ تُضاف جميع البهارات مع الاستمرار بالتحريك. تُرفع المقلاة عن النار، ويُضاف الصنوبر المحمص، يُحرّك الخليط ويُترَك جانبًا حتى يبرد.

نصيحتي لعمل الكبة التي تعلّمتها من أمي، هي العمل بأيدٍ مبلّلة بالماء البارد: نأخذ كرة من العجين وبمساعدة الإبهام نعمل بها حفرة ونقوم بلفها ببطء لتكبير الحفرة، ثم نحشوها بواسطة ملعقة صغيرة، وأخيرًا نغلقها ونُشكّل الكبة على شكل بيضوي. يجب أن يكون سُمك العجينة 2 سم وبدون فتحات.

بعد حشو جميع أقراص الكبة، تُقلَى في زيت عميق ساخن. يجب أن يكون الزيت ساخنًا جدًّا وإلاّ ستتفتّت الكبة أثناء القلي. تُقلى الأقراص لمدة 2-3 دقائق حتى يصبح لونها داكنًا.

### لوصفة صحيّة أكثر

لمن يتفادون القلي يمكن خبز الكبة في فرن مسخّن مسبقًا على حرارة 180 درجة، لمدة عشر دقائق حتى يصبح لونها داكنًا. خذوا بالاعتبار أن مذاق الكبة المخبوزة مختلف عن المقلية.

To check that the oil is hot enough – first fry one kubeh, as a test.

**TIP!**

للتأكد من أن درجة حرارة الزيت ملائمة للقلي: اقلوا قرصًا واحدًا فقط للتجربة.

# MANAQISH WO LABANE
## PITA WITH ZA'ATAR AND LABANE
### المناقيش واللبنة

This dish brings to my mind the blue sky, the smell of the fresh mountain air, and the memory of sitting under an olive tree, dipping a fresh manaqushe in labane cheese – my village saturating my soul. Manaqushe (plural: manaqish) is a wonderful pastry that the name "za'atar pita" doesn't do justice. And what can be better than a manaqushe slathered with labane? But now, as a vegan, I can't be faithful to the original. Rather than bringing the village to me, I have to bring my new life to the village with a gorgeous, healthy and completely vegan labane. Almonds, cashews, garlic, and olive oil are flavors that make you want to sit again under the old olive tree, dreaming.

# INGREDIENTS

(Makes 8 units)

### MANAQISH

3 cups flour
1 tablespoon dry yeast
1 tablespoon brown sugar
1 teaspoon Himalayan (or regular)
salt
1 cup tepid water

### TOPPING

1 cup za'atar, preferably fresh
½ cup olive oil

### LABANE

1 cup peeled, raw almonds,
   soaked overnight
½ cup raw cashews, soaked overnight
½ cup dried soy beans, soaked overnight
¼ cup olive oil
Juice from 2 large lemons
1 garlic clove
2 cups water
About ½ teaspoon salt

# PREPARATION

### FOR THE MANAQISH

Preheat the oven to 200 degrees C
(400 degrees F). In a large bowl, mix all of the
dry ingredients. Add the water gradually while
kneading. Knead the dough for 10 more minutes,
until it's firm. Cover with shrink wrap and a clean
towel, and let the dough rest until it doubles in
volume – 60-90 minutes in summer, 2-3 hours in
winter.
Spread flour on a clean surface and knead the
dough, letting all the air out. Cut into 8 equal
parts and form balls. Roll out to the desired
size (I recommend about 15 cm (6 inches) in
diameter). Cover with a towel and let rest for 10
more minutes.
In a bowl, mix the olive oil and za'atar.
Using your fingertips, lightly press the surfaces
of the pitas (to keep them from inflating). Brush
each of them with olive oil and za'atar to taste.
Take the oven down to 180 degrees C (350
degrees F), lightly oil a baking pan and arrange
the pitas on it. Make sure to keep them about 2
cm (1 inches) apart. Bake for 10 minutes, or until
the inner part is light brown.

### FOR THE LABANE

Use a food processor to blend all of the
ingredients except for the water and salt. Add
the water gradually while processing, until you
reach your preferred texture. Keep in mind that
the labane is meant to be relatively thick, but it
tends to get thicker when refrigerated. Add the
salt, taste and adjust seasoning. I recommend
that you taste and adjust the seasoning again
after refrigerating.
The manaqish is served on a wooden or straw
tray with a plate of labane garnished with olive
oil, olives and fresh vegetables.

In winter, it's best served with a
cup of aromatic herbal tea, for the
complete experience.

**TIP!**

في الشتاء تُقدَّم مع شاي الأعشاب لمذاق متكامل.

## طريقة التحضير

### المناقيش

تُخلَط مواد العجينة الجافة أولاً، ثمّ يُضاف الماء بالتدريج أثناء العجن لمدة 10 دقائق تقريبًا حتى نحصل على عجينة طرية ومتماسكة. تُغلَّف العجينة بنايلون وتُغطَّى بفوطة نظيفة وتُترَك لترتاح ويتضاعف حجمها – بالصيف بين ساعة لساعة ونصف، وبالشتاء بين ساعتين ونصف حتى ثلاث ساعات.

يُخرَج الهواء من العجينة من خلال الضغط عليها، ثمّ تُقطَّع إلى 8 كرات. تُفرَد الكرات بالشوبك إلى دوائر سُمكها 2 سم، يُراعَى رشّ الطحين حتى لا تلتصق العجينة بسطح العمل ثم تُغطَّى لترتاح لمدة 10 دقائق أخرى.

### لتحضير المناقيش

يُخلَط الزيت والزعتر ويُسخَّن الفرن إلى حرارة 200 درجة.
يُضغط على وجه العجينة برفق بأطراف الأصابع حتى لا تنتفخ أثناء الخبز، وتُدهَن بمقدار من مزيج الزعتر والزيت حسب الرغبة. تُرتَّب المناقيش على صينية مدهونة بالقليل من الزيت، مع الحفاظ على بعد 2 سم فيما بينها. تُخفَّف حرارة الفرن إلى 180 درجة وتُخبَز المناقيش لمدة 10 دقائق أو حتى تصبح أطرافها ذهبية اللون.

### اللبنة

تُخلَط جميع المكوّنات، ما عدا الماء والملح، في الخلاط الكهربائي.
يُضاف الماء بالتدريج حتى نحصل على القوام المناسب، مع الأخذ بعين الاعتبار أن اللبنة تجمد في الثلاجة. أخيرًا يُضاف الملح. يمكن تعديل التوابل إذا لزم الأمر لتحسين المذاق.
تُقدَّم المناقيش على صينية من الخشب أو القش لمنظر قروي مثير للشهيّة (اختياري) بجانب طبق اللبنة المطيّبة بزيت الزيتون، والزيتون البيتي.

## المقادير
(لـ 8 أقراص)

### للمناقيش
3 كوب طحين
1 ملعقة كبيرة خميرة فورية
1 ملعقة كبيرة سكر بني
1 ملعقة صغيرة ملح
1 كوب ماء فاتر

### للزعتر
1 كوب زعتر طازج
½ كوب زيت زيتون

### اللبنة
1 كوب لوز مقشر غير محمص منقوع لليلة
½ كوب كاجو غير محمص منقوع لليلة
½ كوب فول الصويا منقوع لليلة
¼ كوب زيت زيتون
عصير 2 حبة ليمون كبيرة
1 فص ثوم
2 كوب ماء
½ ملعقة صغيرة ملح

39

# MOGHRABIEH PALESTINIAN COUSCOUS WITH CHICKPEA STEW

المغربية

For me, this cozy winter dish is shrouded in childhood memories – the cold air, the steaming kitchen, and mom's voice, calling us to come because the moghrabieh is ready, and hurry so it won't get cold... It is a stew of maftoul – bulgur and flour, so named because of the twisting, circular gestures used to prepare it on the work surface – with warm chickpeas, a lot of onion and a steaming broth. In this version I omitted the chicken from the original recipe. The rest is completely traditional, if you insist on preparing the maftoul yourself.
Ready-made maftoul can also be found in middle-eastern shops, and if you can't find it – you can also use Israeli couscous. The children would certainly like it.

# INGREDIENTS

(Serves 4-6)

HOMEMADE MAFTOUL

2 cups bulgur wheat, cooked
About 1 cup flour

STEW

2 cups chickpeas, soaked overnight
1 teaspoon baking soda
½ kg (1 pound) homemade maftoul,
 or 2 cups Israeli couscous
2 liters (half a gallon) vegetable stock
 (see recipe on page 161)
2 large onions, quartered
2 teaspoon cumin
1 teaspoon red paprika
1 teaspoon dry garlic powder
Salt and pepper

# PREPARATION

FOR THE HOMEMADE MAFTOUL

Spread about a spoonful of bulgur on a large,
clean, surface. Sprinkle a bit of flour on top, wet
your hands and, using circular motions, mix the
bulgur and flour with your fingertips, not pressing
too hard, until all of the bulgur is well coated
with flour. Make sure to work patiently and not to
rush. Rather than large balls of dough, you want
to create very small balls of flour-coated bulgur.
Repeat with all of the bulgur and flour, using
small quantities each time.

FOR THE STEW

Strain the chickpeas, pour in a deep pan and
cover with water. Add the baking soda and cook
over medium heat for an hour, until partially
soft. Strain again. Put the prepared maftoul in
a metal strainer and cover. In a deep pot boil
the vegetable stock, onion and spices. Put the
maftoul strainer over the pot and steam for 20
minutes, until the maftoul is cooked and the
onion is soft. Let the maftoul cool for a bit, and
separate it using a fork. If you are using store-
bought Israeli couscous, prepare it according to
the instructions. Add the chickpeas and maftoul
to the soup and cook it for 5-7 more minutes.
To serve, place the chickpeas in a deep bowl,
spoon the maftoul and onion over them and pour
a generous helping of soup on top.

المقادير

(لـ 4-6 وجبات)

المفتول - وصفة أساسيّة

2 كوب برغل خشن
طحين أبيض (حتى مقدار كوب واحد)

للمغربية

2 كوب حمص حب منقوع ليلة كاملة
1 ملعقة صغيرة بيكربونات الصودا
¼ كيلوغرام مفتول جاهز من
 الوصفة الأساسيّة أو 2 كوب كسكس
2 لتر مرق خضار (الوصفة صفحة 161)
2 بصلة كبيرة مقطعة لأرباع
2 ملعقة صغيرة كمون
1ملعقة صغيرة ببريكا حلوة
1 ملعقة بهار بودرة الثوم
ملح وفلفل أسود حسب الرغبة

طريقة التحضير

المفتول

نضع حفنة من البرغل على سطح نظيف وكبير للعمل، وننثر فوقها
القليل من الطحين. نبلّل اليدين ونخلط البرغل والطحين معا بأطراف
الأصابع بصورة دائرية، حتى تتغطى حبات البرغل بالطحين. من المهم
العمل ببطء حتى لا تتكون كتل صغيرة من الطحين والماء، وإذا تكوّنت
يمكن التخلص منها بواسطة المنخل. نكرّر العملية عدة مرات حتى تفرغ
كمية البرغل.

المغربية

تُصفى حبوب الحمص من الماء وتوضَع في قدر كبيرة مع الماء وكربونات
الصودا وتُطهى على نار متوسطة لمدة ساعة، حتى تشرف على النضج.
يُوضَع المفتول في وعاء خاص للطبخ على البخار ويُغطّى. في قدر عميقة
يُغلى مرق الخضار مع البصل والبهارات، ويُوضَع فوقه وعاء المفتول،
ونواصل الطهي لمدة 20 دقيقة حتى يطرى البصل ويجهز المفتول. يُوضع
المفتول جانبًا حتى يبرد قليلا، ويُحرّك قليلاً بالشوكة كيلا يلتصق.
إذا استعملتم الكسكس الجاهز بدلاً من المفتول، فاتّبعوا التعليمات
الواردة على الغلاف. يُوضع المفتول والحمص في قدر المرق مع البصل
ويُطهى لمدة 5-7 دقائق أخرى.
يُوضَع الحمص في طبق عميق ويُضاف إليه المفتول والبصل ثم يُسكَب
فوقه المرق.

# INGREDIENTS

(Serves 4-6)

## COUSCOUS

4 cups vegetable stock
   (see recipe on page 161)
2 medium sized sweet potatoes,
   peeled and diced
2 cups couscous, uncooked
2 tablespoon olive oil
Salt

## LOUBIEH

1 kg (2.2 lbs) green loubieh pods,
   fresh or frozen
¼ cup olive oil
½ onion, diced
2 garlic cloves, crushed
Salt and pepper

# PREPARATION

## FOR THE COUSCOUS

In a deep pot, bring the vegetable stock to a boil,
add the sweet potatoes and a pinch of salt, and
cook for half an hour.
In a bowl, mix the couscous with the olive oil and
a pinch of salt. Pour in a steam-cooker strainer
and place over the pot for 15 minutes.
Use a fork to fluff the couscous, gently breaking
down any lumps. Steam for 10 more minutes.

## FOR THE LOUBIEH

Wash the loubieh, take the ends off and cut each
pod into thirds.
In a wide pan, heat one tablespoon of olive oil,
add the onion and garlic and fry until golden.
Add the rest of the olive oil and the loubieh
and sauté for 5 minutes while gently stirring.
Add half a cup of water, season with salt and
pepper, cover and cook over medium heat for 20
minutes, until the loubieh turns bright green.
Serve layered in a deep plate - first the
couscous, then the loubieh and sweet potatoes,
and finally pour the soup over everything.

---

# المقادير

(لـ 4-6 وجبات)

## الكسكس

4 كوب مرق خضار
(الوصفة صفحة 161)
2 حبة بطاطا حلوة مقشّرة
ومقطّعة لمكعبات
2 كوب كسكس ناعم
2 ملعقة كبيرة زيت زيتون
ملح

## اللوبيا

1 كيلو لوبيا طازجة أو مثلجة
¼ كوب زيت زيتون
½ بصلة مقطّعة لمكعبات
2 فص ثوم مهروس
ملح وفلفل أسود حسب الرغبة

# طريقة التحضير

## الكسكس

يُغلى مرق الخضار في قدر، وتُضاف إليه مكعبات البطاطا الحلوة ورشة
ملح، ويُترك على نار متوسطة لمدة نصف ساعة.
يُخلَط الكسكس مع الزيت ورشّة ملح، ويُطهى على بخار مرق الخضار
مع البطاطا بواسطة مصفاة خاصة لمدة ربع ساعة. يُحرّك الكسكس
حتى لا يلتصق، ويُطهى لمدة 10 دقائق أخرى.

## اللوبيا

تُغسل اللوبيا، ويُزال الخيط من جوانبها ويُقطَّع كل قرن إلى ثلاث قطع.
تُقلى قطع البصل والثوم في قدر مع مقدار ملعقة كبيرة من الزيت حتى
يصبح لونها ذهبيًّا. يُضاف باقي الزيت واللوبيا وتُحرَّك المحتويات لمدة
5 دقائق. يُسكَب في القدر نصف كوب ماء، ويُنثَر الملح والفلفل الأسود.
تُغطَّى القدر وتُترَك على نار متوسطة لمدة 20 دقيقة حتى تذبل اللوبيا.
يُسكَب الكسكس في طبق عميق وتُضاف إليه اللوبيا والبطاطا الحلوة
وبعض المرق.

# LOUBIEH BLACK-EYED PEA PODS & COUSCOUS
## اللوبيا والكسكس

There are many ways to cook loubieh – in a rich tomato sauce, served with pitas and hummus, or, as in this recipe, sautéed in olive oil. Either way, they're green, juicy and healthy, and go wonderfully with couscous. If you can't find fresh loubieh, you can substitute with green beans.

# BASBUSE/HARISE | البسبوسة أو الهريسة

A terrific vegan version of the traditional semolina cake, which usually contains milk and honey, and occasionally eggs. This sweet cake is the star of our (and especially my) special occasions, such as holidays, engagements, successful exams, or passing a driver's license test (even if it was the tenth try). A delight to coconut lovers – in many recipes there isn't any, but in this one it dominates.

# INGREDIENTS

(Makes 1 16X22 cm [6X8½ inch] baking dish)

BASBUSE

2 cups fine semolina
1½ cups non-dairy milk,
    preferably unsweetened almond
1 cup sweet soy yoghurt, homemade
    (see recipe on page 162) or store-bought
¼ cup sugar
1½ cups shredded coconut
1 tablespoon coconut oil
1 tablespoon baking powder
2 tablespoon rose water
30 halved bleached almonds

QATAR (SUGAR) SYRUP

2 cups brown sugar
1 cup water
1 tablespoon lemon juice
1 tablespoon rose water

# PREPARATION

FOR THE BASBUSE

Preheat the oven to 180 degrees C (350 degrees F). In a large bowl, mix all of the ingredients except for the almonds and knead well until the texture is uniform. Transfer the mixture to an oiled baking dish and flatten with your hands or a blunt knife. Place the almonds on top, about 3 cm (1½ inches) apart. Bake for 35 minutes, until the cake is light brown. To check if the cake is ready, stick a toothpick into it. If the toothpick comes out dry, the cake is ready.

FOR THE QATAR SYRUP

Cook the sugar and water over low heat until the sugar completely dissolves. Add the lemon juice and rose water and stir continuously until it boils. Lower the heat and cook for 15 more minutes. Cut the cake into rectangles while still hot, and pour an even layer of syrup over them. Serve hot or cold, with spearmint tea or black coffee.

# المقادير

(لصينية فرن 22×16 سم)

عجينة البسبوسة

2 كوب سميد ناعم
1½ كوب حليب نباتي,
مفضل حليب لوز غير محلّى
1 كوب لبن صويا محلّى، صنع بيتي
(انظروا الوصفة صفحة 162) أو جاهز
¼ كوب سكر
1½ كوب جوز هند مطحون
1 ملعقة كبيرة زيت جوز الهند
1 ملعقة كبيرة باكينج باودر
2 ملعقة ماء زهر
30 حبة لوز مقطّعة لأنصاف

القطر

2 كوب سكر بنّي
1 كوب ماء
1 ملعقة كبيرة عصير ليمون
1 ملعقة كبيرة ماء زهر

# طريقة التحضير

البسبوسة

تُخلَط مكوّنات البسبوسة (دون اللوز) في وعاء كبير وتُعجَن جيّدًا باليدين حتى الحصول على قوام متجانس. تُوضَع العجينة في صينية الفرن مدهونة بقليل من الزيت، ويتم توزيعها على الصينية من خلال الضغط برفق باليدين. تُوزَّع أنصاف اللوز على وجه العجينة مع الحفاظ على بعد 3 سم فيما بينها.

تُخبَز البسبوسة في فرن مسخّن مسبقًا على حرارة 180 درجة لمدة 35 دقيقة حتى تصبح ذهبيّة أو بنيّة اللون. نغرز عودًا خشبيًا في منتصف الصينية فإذا خرج جافًا نعرف أن البسبوسة قد نضجت.

القطر

يُغلَى الماء مع السكر على نار متوسطة حتى الذوبان، ثم يُضاف عصير الليمون وماء الزهر ويُحرّك حتى يغلي. تُخفَّف النار ويُترك المزيج ليغلي على نار هادئة لمدة ربع ساعة.

تُقطَّع البسبوسة وهي ساخنة إلى مربعات متساوية بحيث يكون في منتصف كل قطعة نصف حبة لوز، ثم يُسكَب عليها القطر. تُقدَّم ساخنة أو باردة مع الشاي بالنعناع أو القهوة.

# INGREDIENTS

(Serves 4)

1 liter non-dairy milk, preferably oat
¼ cup sugar
1 tablespoon corn starch
2 cups thin, short soup noodles

GARNISH
Cut fruit
Raisins
Crushed walnuts and almonds
Rose water

# PREPARATION

In a deep pan heat the milk and sugar over medium heat. Stir until the sugar is completely dissolved.
Add the noodles to the pot and cook over low heat, stirring constantly for 15-20 minutes until the noodles are soft.
Dissolve the corn starch in a ¼ cup of cold water, add to the noodles and cook, stirring continuously, for 5 minutes until the mixture thickens.
Pour the sweet noodles into serving cups and garnish according to taste. Refrigerate overnight. Serve cold.

المقادير

(لـ 4 وجبات)

1 لتر حليب نباتي, مفضل حليب الشوفان
¼ كوب سكر
1 ملعقة كبيرة نشاء
2 كوب شعيرية دقيقة
وقصيرة للشوربة

للتزيين
فواكه مقطعة
زبيب
جوز ولوز مطحون خشن
القليل من ماء الورد

طريقة التحضير

يُسخَّن الحليب والسكر في قدر عميقة على نار متوسطة ويُحرّك المزيج حتى الذوبان.
تُضاف الشعيرية إلى القدر ويُطهى الخليط على نار هادئة، مع مواصلة التحريك، لمدة 15-20 دقيقة، حتى تطرى الشعيرية.
يُذوَّب النشاء في ربع كوب من الماء البارد، ثم يُضاف إلى قدر الحليب مع الاستمرار بالتحريك لمدة خمس دقائق حتى يصبح متماسكًا.
يُسكَب الخليط في كؤوس التقديم الشخصية ويُزيَّن حسب الرغبة. تُترَك الكؤوس ليلة في البراد وتُقدَّم باردة.

# SH'IRIEH BIL HELIB
## NOODLE PUDDING

الشعيرية بالحليب

It takes 15 minutes to prepare this sweet, but you still have to wait a whole night to eat it... Noodle pudding and its variant – rice pudding - are beloved desserts of the Arab cuisine, traditionally served during the month of Ramadan. In my family we used to eat this wonderful delicacy during the pre-dawn meal before the fast, to start the day with a sweet and energetic feeling. But you can also adopt this recipe on other days, including Sunday mornings when you want to pamper yourself.

## QATAYEF | القطايف

A famous sweet pastry of the Arab cuisine, mostly enjoyed during the month of Ramadan. The batter is prepared the same way as pancake batter, and there are many versions of the filling. Qatayef always reminds me of the festive break-fast meals with my extended family, the sweetness of the aftertaste, the dribbling syrup and the cold drink that comes with it.

# INGREDIENTS

(Makes 10 units)

2 cups flour
½ cup fine semolina
3 tablespoon baking powder
¼ teaspoon baking soda
¼ cup brown sugar
3 cups water

QATAR (SUGAR) SYRUP

2 cups brown sugar
1 cup water
1 tablespoon lemon juice
1 tablespoon rose water

FILLING

1 cup ground nuts
1 tablespoon cinnamon
2 tablespoon brown sugar
¼ cup raisins
Deep-frying oil
(1 tablespoon to cook the batter and
enough to deep fry the qatayef).

# PREPARATION

FOR THE BATTER

In a bowl, mix the flour, semolina, baking powder
and baking soda.
In another bowl dissolve the brown sugar in the
water. Add the wet mixture to the dry and mix
until uniform. Cover with shrink wrap and let rest
at room temperature for 15 minutes.
Heat a non-stick pan and oil it with a paper
towel. With a ladle, pour the batter into the pan,
creating circles 10 cm (4 inches) in diameter.
Fry until bubbles form. Flip and fry for 2 more
minutes. In the same manner, prepare all of the
batter.

FOR THE QATAR SYRUP

Cook the sugar and water over low heat until the
sugar completely dissolves. Add the lemon juice
and rose water and mix until boiling. Lower the
heat and cook for 15 more minutes.

FOR FILLING AND FRYING

In a bowl, mix all of the ingredients for the filling.
Put a spoonful of the filling in the middle of each
circle of dough, close into half-moons and pinch
closed, about 2 cm (4/5 inch) from the edge.
In a pot, heat the deep-frying oil and carefully fry
the filled qatayef for 3-4 minutes, until brown.
Dip in the qatar syrup and put on a paper towel.
Serve hot with a cold drink.

## المقادير

(لـ 10 اقراص)

### للعجينة

2 كوب طحين
½ كوب سميد ناعم
3 ملعقة صغيرة باكينج باودر
¼ ملعقة صغيرة بيكربونات الصودا
¼ كوب سكر بنّي
3 كوب ماء

### القطر

2 كوب سكر بنّي
1 كوب ماء
1 ملعقة كبيرة عصير ليمون
1 ملعقة كبيرة ماء زهر

### للحشوة

1 كوب جوز مطحون خشن
1 ملعقة كبيرة قرفة
2 ملعقة كبيرة سكر بنّي
¼ كوب زبيب

زيت للقلي

## طريقة التحضير

### العجينة

يُذوَّب السكر بالماء وثم يُخلَط مع جميع مكوّنات العجينة (عدا الزيت) حتى تتكوّن عجينة متجانسة ثم تُغلَّف بالنايلون وتُترَك لمدة ربع ساعة في درجة حرارة الغرفة. في مقلاة ساخنة مدهونة بالقليل من الزيت، يُسكَب العجين الرخو بالمغرفة على شكل دوائر قطرها 10 سم وتُترَكَ الأقراص حتى تظهر فقاعات في الجهة العليا. توضع الأقراص جانبًا لتبرد.

### القطر

يُغلى الماء مع السكر حتى الذوبان، يُضاف عصير الليمون وماء الزهر مع الاستمرار بالتحريك حتى يغلي المزيج، ثمّ تُخفَّف الحرارة ويُترَك على نار هادئة لمدة ربع ساعة.

### الحشوة

تُخلَط جميع مكوّنات الحشوة في وعاء. يوضَع مقدار ملعقة صغيرة من الحشوة وسط العجينة، وتُغلق أطرافها على شكل نصف دائرة بالضغط عليها جيّدًا لتلتصق. تُقلَى القطايف في زيت القلي الساخن لمدة 3-4 دقائق حتى تصبح ذهبية أو داكنة اللون، ثم تُغمَر في القطر وتُصفَّى منه بواسطة ورق المطبخ. تُقدَّم القطايف ساخنة مع مشروب بارد.

# FATTOUSH | الفتوش

Fattoush is one of the most joyful, colorful and filling salads the Arab cuisine has to offer, and it's also a handy solution for dry, leftover pitas (here's your excuse to buy more in advance!). Brush them with a bit of olive oil and za'atar, throw them in the oven and you have homemade croutons (a trick that can upgrade other salads as well). The original version of the salad contains hard cheese. Here I replace it with a tasty, easy-to-make vegan version. The nutritional yeast gives it the desired cheese-like flavor. The croutons and vegan cheese should be prepared before the salad, so it can be served as fresh as possible.

# INGREDIENTS

(Serves 4)

FOR THE SALAD

3 medium cucumbers
3 medium, firm tomatoes
1 medium red onion
1 cup spring onion, chopped
3 small radishes
1 small head of lettuce
⅓ cup parsley, chopped
½ spearmint, chopped
¼ cup olive oil
Juice from 1 lemon
1 teaspoon sumac
Salt

FOR THE CROUTONS

1 pita, preferably stale
1 teaspoon za'atar
1 tablespoon olive oil

FOR THE VEGAN CHEESE

¼ cup raw almonds
1 tablespoon dried garlic powder
2 tablespoon nutritional yeast*

# PREPARATION

FOR THE CROUTONS (OPTIONAL)

Preheat the oven to 180 degrees C (350 degrees F). Cut the pita into thick bands and put them in a mixing bowl. Add the olive oil and za'atar and stir until the pitas are thoroughly coated with the mixture. Place the pita bands on a baking dish lined with parchment paper and bake for 15 minutes, or until brown (careful not to burn them).

FOR THE VEGAN CHEESE (OPTIONAL)

In a food processor, blend all of the ingredients until uniform.

FOR THE SALAD

Dice the cucumber, tomatoes and red onion, cut the radishes into thin slices and finely chop the lettuce. Put all the vegetables in a very large bowl and season with the olive oil, lemon juice, sumac and salt. Mix well, taste and adjust seasoning.

FOR SERVING

Arrange the croutons and vegan cheese over the salad and serve immediately.

*Nutritional yeast is a condiment that gives a cheese-like aroma to many vegan dishes. It can be found in natural food stores. Despite the similar name, it should not be confused with baking yeast.

## طريقة التحضير

### السلطة

تُقطَّع حبات الخيار والبندورة والبصل لمربعات وتُقطَّع الفجل لشرائح رفيعة. تُفرم الخسة فرمًا ناعمًا وتُوضَع الخضار في وعاء ويُضاف إليها الزيت والملح وعصير الليمون والسماق وتُخلط جيّدًا. نحسّن التوابل حسب المذاق.

### الخبز المحمص (من المفضل تحضيره قبل السلطة)

يُقطَّع رغيف الخبز بالطول ويوضَع في وعاء، ثم يُضاف إليه الزيت والزعتر ويُخلَط جيّدًا. توضَع شرائح الخبز في صينية فرن مغطاة بورق الخبز وتُدخَل إلى فرن مسخَّن مسبقًا لحرارة 180 درجة لمدة ربع ساعة حتى يصبح ذهبيّ اللون.

### بديل الجبنة (من المفضل تحضيرها قبل السلطة)

تُطحَن مواد بديل الجبنة في الخلاط الكهربائي حتى الحصول على قوام متجانس.

تُسكب السلطة في طبق عميق ويُضاف إليها الخبز المحمص وبديل الجبنة.

### السلطة

3 حبة خيار متوسطة
3 حبة بندورة صلبة متوسطة
1 حبة متوسطة بصل بنفسجي
1 كوب بصل أخضر مفروم
3 رؤوس فجل صغيرة
1 خسة صغيرة
½ كوب بقدونس مفروم
½ كوب نعنع مفروم
¼ كوب زيت زيتون
عصير ليمونة واحدة
1 ملعقة كبيرة سماق
ملح حسب الرغبة

### الخبز المحمص

1 رغيف خبز غير طازج
1 ملعقة صغيرة زعتر
1 ملعقة كبيرة زيت زيتون

### بديل الجبنة

¼ كأس لوز غير محمص
1 ملعقة صغيرة بودرة الثوم
2 ملعقة صغيرة خميرة البيرة*

*خميرة البيرة هي بهار يعطي نكهة الجبنة بالوجبات الخضريّة ويمكن العثور عليه في حوانيت المنتجات الخضرية. بالرغم من انّ الاسم يذكرنا باسم الخميرة العادية، لكن بالواقع لا يوجد علاقة بينهما البتّة.

# WARAK DAWALI
## STUFFED VINE LEAVES
ورق الدوالي

There are some Arab dishes I didn't much like as a child. I only started to appreciate them when I grew up, and especially when I became vegan. With the warak dawali, stuffed vine leaves, it was love at first sight, and improving the recipe is an integral part of our life-long romance. In my experience, this special dish is best prepared when you have time and passion to invest in it, since you can't rush the rolling of the vine leaves.

Ultimately, the dish is well worth the effort – the flavors have an aromatic and slightly sour harmony, and the aesthetic is very impressive. It is sure to elevate the effect of any festive meal. You can purchase fresh vine leaves from greengrocers or middle-eastern shops in season and freeze them for use throughout the year.

# INGREDIENTS

(Makes 45 Units)

45 vine leaves

STUFFING

¾ cup jasmine rice, washed
¼ teaspoon turmeric
¼ teaspoon ground nutmeg
Salt and pepper
2 tomatoes, diced very small
¼ cup vegan mince, homemade
    (see recipe on page 160)
    or store-bought, natural flavor
1 tablespoon olive oil

COOKING

1 medium tomato
3-4 cups vegetable stock
    (see recipe on page 161)
2 tablespoon tomato paste
1 tablespoon olive oil
Juice from 1 large lemon
Salt

# PREPARATION

Take the stems off the leaves, arrange them in a large pot and pour hot water over them until completely covered. Let the leaves soak for ten minutes and gently squeeze the water out.

FOR THE STUFFING

Leaving the rice uncooked, mix all of the ingredients for the stuffing in a bowl.

FOR THE ASSEMBLING

Spread the leaves over the work surface, so the smooth side faces down, the stem side up, and the base of each leaf points towards you. Place a small teaspoon of stuffing on the base of each leaf (adjusting the amount of stuffing to the size of the leaf). Fold the sides on top of the stuffing and roll from the base upwards, to form a 'cigar.'

FOR COOKING

Thinly slice the tomato and arrange at the bottom of the pot. This 'base' will prevent the vine leaves from sticking to the pot and add to their flavor. Arrange the stuffed leaves over the tomato in neat rows and pour 3 cups of vegetable stock over them. Mix the tomato paste, olive oil, lemon juice and salt to taste (one teaspoon or less) in a cup and add to the pot. If the vine leaves aren't completely covered, add another cup of stock. Cover the pot, bring to a boil and cook over medium-low heat for 30-40 minutes, until the water has been absorbed and the vine leaves are soft. Let rest for 20 minutes. Serve with cold vegan yoghurt (recipe on page 162) or tabule salad (recipe on page 78).

## المقادير

(لنصف كيلو ورق عنب/دوالي)

**للحشوة**

¾ كوب أرز الياسمين مغسول ومصفّى

¼ ملعقة صغيرة كركم

¼ ملعقة جوزة الطيب

ملح وفلفل أسود حسب الرغبة

2 حبة بندورة مفرومة ناعمًا

¼ كوب بروتين الصويا المطحون
سواء من صنع بيتي
(الوصفة صفحة 160)
أو جاهز بالنكهة الطبيعية

1 ملعقة كبيرة زيت نباتي

**الدوالي**

1 حبة بندورة متوسّطة

3-4 كوب مرق خضار (الوصفة صفحة 161)

2 ملعقة كبيرة معجون البندورة

1 ملعقة كبيرة زيت زيتون

عصير ليمونة واحدة

ملح حسب الرغبة

## طريقة التحضير

تُنزع أعناق ورق العنب وتُوضع في قدر، يسكب فوقها الماء الساخن ليغمرها تمامًا، تُترك لمدة 10 دقائق ثم تُصفّى.

**الحشوة**

تُخلط جميع مكوّنات الحشوة في وعاء. يُوضع مقدار ملعقة صغيرة من الحشوة على الوجه الخشن لورقة العنب، ثم يُطوى القسم السفلي من الورقة، وبعدها طرفا الورقة لتغطية بقية الحشوة بالكامل، ثم نبدأ اللف من الأسفل للأعلى مع الضغط على الحبة جيّدًا كيلا تخرج الحشوة أثناء الطبخ.

**الدوالي**

تُرتّب شرائح البندورة في قعر القدر وتُصفّ فوقها أوراق العنب المحشوة. يُخلط مرق الخضار مع معجون البندورة، زيت الزيتون، عصير الليمون، الملح والفلفل ويُسكب المزيج في القدر حتى يغمر أوراق العنب. تُترك القدر على نار قوية حتى تبدأ بالغليان، ثم تُخفَّف الحرارة وتُترك لمدة 30-40 دقيقة تقريبًا حتى تطرى الأوراق وتنضج الحشوة. تُترك القدر مغطّاة لمدة 20 دقيقة أخرى بعد إزالتها عن النار، وذلك لامتصاص الصلصة.

تُقدَّم أوراق العنب مع اللبن النباتي البارد (الوصفة صفحة 162) أو مع سلطة التبولة (الوصفة صفحة 78).

TIP!

For softer vine leaves – add another ½-1 cup of the cooking liquid.

للحصول على أوراق طرية جدا يمكن إضافة كوب ونصف من مرق الخضار خلال الطبخ.

# Tel Aviv

# تل ابيب

## The City of Change & Opportunity

## مدينة الإمكانيات والتغييرات

**Photography by** Ella Leshman

61

# Chapter two

# Tel Aviv

تل ابيب

I will never forget my first day of university. With broken Hebrew and big hopes, I began the first semester of my occupational therapy degree. I was twenty. For the first time in my life, I would sleep outside my parents' house. For the first time in my life, I would be completely self-reliant.

I sat in a class composed almost entirely of girls. There was only one male student, an Arab. The lesson began. I tried to listen intently and understand what the professor was saying. Suddenly, he used a Hebrew word that sent me back to the dormitory in tears: "proportional." What was this word? What could it mean? I can't describe the depth of my frustration hearing the unfamiliar word... if this was how the professor spoke in the first lesson, what words would he use in the second? How could I participate in the discussions if I always had to worry about blurting out a sentence in faulty Hebrew?

During those years, I held onto a lot of my anger. I was angry about the foreign language and culture. I was angry about the university and the Jewish students with their flawless Hebrew. Pile on the ever-present anger at the security guards in malls, the humiliating checks on the train, the suspicious and hostile eyes, and you can understand what a storm of negative energy I was.

But then in one class, the lecturer, who I'll never forget, split the class into groups. Whether coincidentally or not, the Arab students gathered in one group alongside some of the Jewish ones.

In one of our discussions, a Jewish student told the male student that, though she didn't hate him, she feared him. Because, she said, any Arab could be a terrorist. He was very hurt by the remark, and it brought my friends to tears. At the next lesson, she apologized whole-heartedly. She was so naïve, she hadn't understood her words to be racist. She told us about her own background, how the constant fear of Arabs was engrained in her education. As she spoke, apologizing repeatedly, she broke into tears.

That day, I decided that it was time for me to also open my heart and finally let go of the fear and the anger. Thanks to that decision, I've been fortunate enough to meet wonderful people. My Hebrew, also, improved with time and practice.

I lived in mesmerizing Tel Aviv for five years – five years of growing into my own personality and empowering myself. I grew into an independent, strong woman. I wanted to swallow the world without even chewing. I collected many memories within the walls of the dormitories and classrooms and among the cafes and hangouts. In Tel Aviv I shed my fear and connected with the other, but I also opened myself up for others to know me without fear or judgment.

In Tel Aviv, this fundamental change in my life took place, and for this reason it will always hold a special place in my heart.

In this chapter, you'll find fun and easy recipes, well suited to the lives of busy students, hopping from papers to exams to work shifts. I hope that each time you prepare one of them, you let go a little bit your own fears. By the end of the chapter, you'll conquer them completely.

# FALAFEL | الفلافل

Falafel is one of the dishes that unite all of us around the dinner table, or more precisely, around the stall... It's tasty, cheap and filling, and you can eat it standing up, to enjoy the tahini dripping off. Here's a chance to bring it home and give it the respect it deserves. This dish is recommended for children's lunch, for family dinners and even for casual friendly get-togethers. Good luck frying, and don't forget to have a lot of napkins ready, as well as good tahini and salads!

# INGREDIENTS

(Makes 40 balls)

1 cup dried chickpeas
1 tablespoon baking soda
¼ cup dried soybeans
¼ cup fresh spinach
    or coriander, chopped
¼ cup parsley, chopped
1 garlic clove
1 teaspoon salt
1 teaspoon cumin
¼ cup breadcrumbs
    (preferably with sesame seeds)
Deep-frying oil

# PREPARATION

Put the chickpeas and baking soda into a pot, cover with cold water and let soak overnight, preferably refrigerated. Put the soybeans in a different pot with cold water and let soak overnight, preferably refrigerated.
Strain the chickpeas and soybeans and blend in a food processor. Add the spinach, parsley, garlic, salt and cumin and blend until uniform. Add the bread crumbs and mix well. The mixture should be soft, but not dry. If it's too dry, add some water (no more then ¼ cup). If it's too liquid, add breadcrumbs. Let rest for 20 minutes. Heat the oil in a large pot or deep fryer. Shape the mixture into balls using your hands or a special falafel spoon and fry in oil until the outside is golden. Carefully take the balls out and leave on a paper towel.
Serve with pitas, salads, pickles and tahini and eat with a lot of love.

Tahini Sauce: Combine ½ cup tahini, ¼ cup cold water, juice from ½ lemon and a teaspoon of salt, and mix until uniform. You can add water or tahini, depending on how thick you want the sauce, or spices and herbs for variety and color.

المقادير

(لـ 40 قرصًا)

1 كوب حب حمص يابس
1 ملعقة صغيرة بيكربونات الصودا
¼ كوب فول الصويا
¼ كوب سبانخ/كزبرة مفروم/ة
¼ كوب بقدونس مفروم
1 فص ثوم مهروس
1 ملعقة صغيرة ملح
1 ملعقة صغيرة كمون
¼ كوب كعك مطحون
    (مفضل مع سمسم)
زيت نباتي للقلي

طريقة التحضير

يُنقَع الحمص بالماء البارد وبيكربونات الصودا في وعاء لمدة 12 ساعة، وفي وعاء آخر يُنقع فول الصويا بالماء البارد دون إضافات لنفس المدة، ثم تُغسَل الحبوب وتُصفّى.
يُطحَن الحمص وفول الصويا، ثم يُضاف السبانخ والبقدونس المفروم والثوم، ويُنثَر عليه الملح والكمون وتُطحَن المحتويات مرة أخرى. يُضاف الكعك المطحون وتُخلط جميع المواد جيّدًا حتى الحصول على عجينة متماسكة وطرية.
إذا كانت العجينة جافة بعض الشيء يُضاف إليها الماء (لا يزيد عن ربع كوب) حتى تطرى، وإذا كانت رخوة يُضاف إليها فتات الخبز حتى الحصول على القوام المناسب. تُترك جانبا لمدة 20 دقيقة. يُسخَّن الزيت في مقلاة، ونقوم بإعداد أقراص الفلافل بواسطة مغرفة الفلافل أو ملعقة طعام مبللة بالماء. يمكن أيضًا استعمال اليدين المبلّلتين بالماء لتكوين أقراص شبه مسطحة. تُقلى أقراص الفلافل حتى تصبح ذهبية اللون ومقرمشة.
تُقدَّم أقراص الفلافل مع أرغفة صغيرة الحجم، صلصة الطحينة، المخللات والسلطات بأنواعها.

# INGREDIENTS

(Serves 4-6)

EGGPLANT

3 medium eggplants
Olive oil

TOMATO SAUCE

1 medium onion, diced
2 tablespoon olive oil
3 fresh tomatoes, diced
2 tablespoon concentrated tomato paste
3 garlic cloves
¼ cup fresh spearmint, chopped
Salt and pepper
1 teaspoon dried garlic powder
¼ cup cooked chickpeas

# PREPARATION

FOR THE EGGPLANT

Preheat oven to 180 degrees C (350 degrees F). Cut the eggplants into slices 1 cm (2/5 inch) thick, lay out on a paper towel and sprinkle salt on both sides. Leave for 20 minutes until the liquid seeps out, and wipe well using a paper towel. Brush with a little olive oil and bake until golden. Turn the slices over and bake for 15-20 more minutes.

FOR THE TOMATO SAUCE

Fry the onion in a deep pan until golden. Add the diced tomatoes, stir and cover. Cook over low heat for about 5 minutes.
Add the tomato paste and a cup of water and stir well. Cover and cook for 10 minutes over low heat. Add garlic and spearmint and season with salt, pepper and garlic powder. Cook for 15 more minutes over low heat.
Add the eggplants to the tomato sauce and stir well. Taste and adjust seasoning as needed. Add the chickpeas and cook over low heat for 20 more minutes.
Serve hot or cold, with tahini, fresh baked bread and a chopped salad.

المقادير

(لـ 4-6 وجبات)

للباذنجان

3حبات باذنجان متوسطة الحجم
زيت زيتون

لصلصة البندورة

1 بصلة متوسطة الحجم مقطّعه لمكعبات
2 ملعقة كبيرة زيت زيتون
3 حبات بندورة ناضجة مقطعة لمكعبات
2 ملعقة كبيرة معجون البندورة
3 فصوص ثوم
¼ كوب نعنع مفروم
ملح وفلفل أسود حسب الرغبة
1ملعقة صغيرة بودرة الثوم
¼ كوب حمص حب مسلوق

طريقة التحضير

الباذنجان

يُقطّع الباذنجان لدوائر سمكها 1سم، يُنثَر على جانبيها الملح وتُوضَع على ورق المطبخ. تُترَك الشرائح جانبا مدة 20 دقيقة حتى تفرز السوائل ثم تُجفَّف بواسطة ورق المطبخ وتُدهَن بالزيت وتُشوى في فرن مسخَّن مسبقا على حرارة 180 درجة لمدة 15-20 دقيقة حتى تبدأ بالاحمرار، ثمّ تُقلَب وتُترك لنفس المدة حتى يحمرّ الوجه الآخر.

صلصة البندورة

يُقلى البصل بالزيت في مقلاة كبيرة حتى يحمرّ، وتُضاف إليه مكعبات البندورة وتُحرّك، ثم تُغطى المقلاة وتُترك على نار هادئة لمدة 5 دقائق. يُضاف معجون البندورة بعد خلطه بكوب من الماء ويُحرّك المزيج جيّدًا ويُترك ليغلي لمدة 10 دقائق على نار هادئة.
يُضاف الثوم والنعنع ويُنثَر الملح والفلفل الأسود وبودرة الثوم. تترك الصلصة لمدة ربع ساعة أخرى على نار هادئة ثمّ يُضاف الباذنجان والحمص. يمكن تعديل المذاق بإضافة التوابل حسب الحاجة. يُحرّك الخليط جيّدًا ثم يُترك لمدة 20 دقيقة أخرى على النار.
تُقدَّم الوجبة مع الطحينة والخبز والسلطة.

Tahini Sauce: Combine ½ cup tahini, ¼ cup cold water, juice from ½ lemon and a teaspoon of salt, and mix until uniform. You can add water or tahini, depending on how thick you want the sauce, or spices and herbs for variety and color.

# MUSAKA'A EGGPLANT IN A MINTY CHICKPEA TOMATO SAUCE

المسقّعة - باذنجان مع صلصة البندورة، الحمص والنعنع

A light, tasty, easy dish of roasted eggplant served in a Mediterranean tomato sauce with spearmint, garlic and chickpeas. Musaka'a means 'cold' in Arabic. This dish is called musaka because it is usually served chilled, having been refrigerated for a whole night to let the flavors come out. You can, of course, serve it hot, but on those scorching summer days, the traditional way is definitely better.

# HOMEMADE HUMMUS | الحمص البيتي

There are countless versions of hummus, and every certified hummus enthusiast is loyal to their regular place – god forbid you should try to tell them to check the joint across the road. Even around making hummus at home, a lot of urban – and rural – myths have been woven, and anyone who has ever made hummus at home is proud of their own secret recipe. Now, you must want to know the secret to my hummus... the truth is there's no secret passed down through the generations, only love and attention to each chickpea. You probably already know that peeling the chickpeas, one by one, is the real secret! Not baking soda while cooking, or ice cubes when grinding. Mind you, if your food processor is strong enough, you can skip the arduous work of peeling and put more effort into the toppings.

I suggest vegan mince for a topping instead of the traditional minced meat, and excellent homemade fava beans to make a complete meal of it. There's no need to fight about it – we're all about peace in the kitchen – but you can at least invent your own hummus-making legends.

# INGREDIENTS

(Serves 2-4)

### HUMMUS

2 cups dried chickpeas,
  preferably very small
1 tablespoon coarse salt
½ teaspoon baking soda
¾ cup tahini
Juice from ½ small lemon
1 garlic clove
1 teaspoon salt

### TOPPING

¼ cup vegan mince, homemade
  (see recipe on page 160) or store-bought
¼ teaspoon sweet paprika
¼ teaspoon dried garlic powder
1 tablespoon olive oil
Salt and pepper
50 g roasted pine nuts
Some cooked chickpeas
Olive oil

# PREPARATION

### FOR THE HUMMUS

Sprinkle the bottom of a large pot with a spoonful of coarse salt. Add the chickpeas to the pot. Cover with a lot of water and let soak overnight (or for at least 8 hours). In summer, it's best to keep them in the refrigerator, but in winter you can leave them out. I also recommend that you change the water after a few hours. Strain the chickpeas, cover with 2 liters of water and cook without salt – bring to a boil, lower the heat a little and let the chickpeas cook for about an hour, until they're slightly soft. Make sure to remove the white foam that surfaces every few minutes. Add baking soda and cook until soft, for about an hour to 90 minutes (depending on the kind of chickpeas). Add water if needed (the water should completely cover the chickpeas). Add some salt and cook for another 30 minutes, until the chickpeas are very soft. To check if they're ready, try squashing them with your hand. If you can do it easily – they're ready. Refrigerate the cooked chickpeas and peel the skins off for a smoother texture (if you have a strong enough food processor, you can skip this part). Keep 1 cup of the cooking water, and strain the chickpeas. Put some of the cooked chickpeas on the side, for garnish. Blend the chickpeas in a food processor with the cup of cooking water and an ice cube (optional, but improves the texture) and gradually add tahini, lemon juice, garlic and salt. Process until smooth. Taste and adjust seasoning.

### FOR THE SERVING

In a non-stick pan, fry the vegan mince with the olive oil and spices. Serve the hummus in deep plates and add some of the vegan mince to each plate. Sprinkle roasted pine nuts, add the chickpeas you saved and pour a generous amount of olive oil.

## المقادير

### للحمص

2 كوب حمص صغير الحبة
1 ملعقة كبيرة ملح خشن
½ ملعقة صغيرة بيكربونات الصودا
¾ كوب طحينة
عصير نصف ليمونة صغيرة
1 فص ثوم مقشّر
1 ملعقة صغيرة ملح

### للتقديم

¼ كوب بروتين الصويا المطحون سواء من صنع بيتي
(انظروا الوصفة صفحة 160)
أو جاهز بالنكهة الطبيعية
¼ ملعقة صغيرة ببريكا حلوة
¼ ملعقة صغيرة بودرة ثوم
1 ملعقة كبيرة زيت زيتون
للقلي
ملح وفلفل أسود حسب الرغبة
50 غرام صنوبر محمص
حفنة من حبوب الحمص المسلوقة
زيت زيتون للتقديم

## طريقة التحضير

### الحمص

يُنقَع الحمص بالماء مع الملح الخشن ليلة كاملة، أو على الأقل ثماني ساعات. يُستحسن تبديل الماء بعد بضع ساعات.
يُغسَل الحمص ويُسلَق في قدر كبيرة من الماء (2 لتر على الأقل) حتى الغليان، ثم تُخفَّف النار ونواصل السلق لمدة ساعة حتى تطرى حبات الحمص. من المهم خلال عملية السلق إزالة الرغوة. تُضاف بعدها بيكربونات الصودا للقدر، ويُترك الحمص على النار لمدة تتراوح بين ساعة ونصف وساعة أخرى حتى ينضج تماما (يتعلق بنوع الحمص). نضيف الماء إذا تبخّر. يُضاف القليل من الملح ويُسلق الحمص لنصف ساعة أخرى حتى نرى أنه صار طريًا تمامًا.
نحتفظ بنصف كوب من ماء السلق، ثم نزيل القشرة عن الحبوب بعد أن تبرد ونحتفظ ببعضها للتزيين.
يُضرب الحمص في الخلاط الكهربائي مع الثوم ونصف كوب من ماء السلق، وتُضاف إليه بالتدريج الطحينة، عصير الليمون، الملح ومكعب الثلج للحصول على قوام ناعم ومتماسك. يُعدَّل المذاق بإضافة الليمون والملح حسب الحاجة.

### الإضافات والتقديم

يُقلى البروتين النباتي مع القليل من الزيت والبهارات في مقلاة غير لاصقة. يُسكب الحمص في طبق عميق، ويُضاف إليه البروتين النباتي، ويُزيّن بالصنوبر وحبوب الحمص المسلوقة وزيت الزيتون؛ تُقَدّم الوجبة كنوع من أنواع المقبّلات اللذيذة.

# INGREDIENTS

(Serves 2-4)

2 cups dried fava beans, preferably small
1 tablespoon baking powder
Juice of ½ large lemon
1 garlic clove
1½ teaspoon salt

GARNISH BEANS

Olive oil
Sweet paprika

# PREPARATION

FOR THE BEANS

Soak the fava beans in water overnight, at least. Wash and strain. Put the strained beans and the baking powder in a pot with a lot of water (about 2 liters, or half a gallon) and bring to a boil. Remove the white foam and cook for an hour to 90 minutes, until the fava beans are very soft. Add water as needed. Cool the pot, keep about half a cup of the cooking water and strain. At this point you can remove the skins, but you can also leave them on. In a food processor, blend the cooked beans with the cooking water you kept and the rest of the ingredients until smooth.

SERVING

Arrange in deep plates, pour olive oil on top and sprinkle with sweet paprika. Serve with fresh homemade pitas, onion and pickles.

## المقادير

(لـ 2-4 وجبات)

### للفول

2 كوب حب فول يابس وصغير
1 ملعقة كبيرة باكينج باودر
عصير نصف ليمونة كبيرة
1½ ملعقة صغيرة ملح

### للتقديم

زيت زيتون
بريكا حلوة

## طريقة التحضير

### تحضير الفول

يُنقع الفول بالماء ليلة كاملة، ثم يُغسل ويُصفّى. يُسلق الفول في قدر تحتوي على 2 لتر ماء على الأقل، ويضاف إليه الباكينج باودر، لمدة تتراوح بين ساعة وساعة ونصف حتى ينضج تمامًا. نضيف المزيد من الماء إذا تبخر. من المهم خلال عملية السلق إزالة الرغوة، وفي نهاية العملية الاحتفاظ بنصف كوب من ماء السلق. يُصفّى الفول ويُقشَّر (غير إلزامي ولكن مستحسن)، ثم يُطحَن أو يُهرَس مع نصف كوب من ماء السلق، ويُضاف إليه عصير الليمون والملح.

### تقديم الفول

يُسكب الفول في طبق عميق ويُضاف إليه زيت الزيتون والبريكا. يُقدَّم مع البصل الأخضر أو الأبيض والخبز الساخن.

TIP!

To save time, you can cook the chickpeas and fava beans at the same time, and serve them together.

من المستحسن سلق الحمص والفول في نفس الوقت لتقليص مدة الطبخ. وتقديم الوجبتين معًا.

# MANTI TURKISH DUMPLINGS

# المانتي

The manti, steamed dumplings stuffed with minced meat, traveled to the Arab cuisine from the traditional Turkish kitchen. My manti is a modern version, vegan, fresh and colorful, with vegan mince replacing the meat and served with vegan, homemade yoghurt. If you're expecting a lot of guests, you better multiply the quantities.

# INGREDIENTS

(Makes 10 dumplings)

### DOUGH

2 cups flour
½ cup water
⅓ cup oil
¼ teaspoon turmeric
1 teaspoon salt

### FILLING

1 tablespoon olive oil
½ cup vegan mince, homemade
  (see recipe on page 160) or store-bought
½ teaspoon sweet paprika
¼ teaspoon dried garlic powder
Salt and pepper

### SERVING

2 tomatoes, blanched and pureed
Coarse salt
Ground black pepper
¼ cup cold sour yoghurt
  (see recipe on page 162)
2 tablespoon pine nuts
1 tablespoon pesto

# PREPARATION

### FOR THE DOUGH

Preheat oven to 180 degrees C (350 degrees F). In a large bowl, mix all of the ingredients until the texture is uniform. Cover and refrigerate for 30 minutes.

### FOR THE STUFFING

Heat the olive oil in a non-stick pan and fry the vegan mince and spices.

### FOR THE DUMPLINGS

Take the dough out of the refrigerator and divide it into 10 small balls. Shape each ball into a 'boat.' Using your pinky, create a hole in the middle of the boat and pinch the sides with your thumb and forefinger. Put a little stuffing in each ball. The dumplings stay open.
Oil a baking dish (or use parchment paper). Arrange the dumplings in rows and bake for 15 minutes, or until the dumplings are brown.

### FOR THE SERVING

Pour the tomato puree into the serving dish, and sprinkle some coarse salt and ground black pepper over it. Put the dumplings over the puree paste and pour cold yoghurt over them. Sprinkle roasted pine nuts and drops of fresh pesto, and serve as a starter or as a side with the main dish.

**Tahini Sauce:** Combine ½ cup tahini, ¼ cup cold water, juice from ½ lemon and a teaspoon of salt, and mix until uniform. You can add water or tahini, depending on how thick you want the sauce, or spices and herbs for variety and color.

## طريقة التحضير

تُخلَط مكوّنات العجينة وتُعجَن حتى تصبح متماسكة ومتجانسة، ثم تُغلَّف بالنايلون وتُترَك في الثلاجة لمدة نصف ساعة.

### الحشوة

يُقلى بروتين الصويا مع القليل من الزيت والبهارات في مقلاة غير لاصقة.

### العجينة

يُقطَّع العجين إلى 10 قطع متساوية، ويُصنع من كل قطعة شكل بيضوي يشبه القارب، نضغط بواسطة البنصر على وسط القارب لنشكّل حفرة، ثمّ نضغط على أطراف القارب بواسطة الابهام والسبابة لنكوّن الحواف. في وسط كل قارب تُوضع ملعقة صغيرة من الحشوة. تُترك القوارب مفتوحة من الأعلى.
تُوضَع الأقراص في صينية مدهونة بالزيت أو مغطاة بورق الخبز، وتُخبَز في فرن مسخّن مسبقًا على حرارة 180 درجة لمدة ربع ساعة، حتى تصبح ذهبيّة اللون.

### التقديم

يُوضع في طبق التقديم هريس البندورة ويُنثر عليه الملح والفلفل الأسود الخشن، ثم تُرتَّب فوقه أقراص المانتي واللبن النباتي وتُزيَّن بالصنوبر المحمّص وصلصة البيستو. تُقدَّم كطبق رئيسي أو ثانوي.

## المقادير

(لـ 10 أقراص)

### للعجينة

2 كوب طحين
½ كوب ماء
⅓ كوب زيت
¼ ملعقة صغيرة كركم
1 ملعقة صغيرة ملح

### للحشوة

1 ملعقة كبيرة زيت زيتون
½ كوب بروتين الصويا المطحون سواء من صنع بيتي (الوصفة صفحة 160) أو جاهز بالنكهة الطبيعية
½ ملعقة صغيرة ببريكا حلوة
¼ ملعقة صغيرة بودرة الثوم
فلفل أسود وملح حسب الرغبة

### للتقديم

2 حبة بندورة مقشّرة ومهروسة
ملح خشن حسب الرغبة
فلفل أسود خشن حسب الرغبة
¼ كوب لبن نباتي (الوصفة صفحة 162)
2 ملعقة كبيرة صنوبر محمّص
1 ملعقة كبيرة صلصة بيستو

**Variation:** You can replace the yoghurt with tahini, or use both.

للتنويع: يمكن استبدال اللبن النباتي بالطحينة. أو تقديم كلتا الإضافتين معًا.

# TABULE SALAD | سلطة التبولة

Careful – addictive dish ahead!
The tabule salad originates in the rich Lebanese cuisine. Recipes vary in the amount of bulgur used and whether tomatoes are included (some don't use them). I prefer a version that doesn't skimp on Bulgur and doesn't use tomatoes, but you can adjust the salad to your liking. At our house, by the way, the tabule always came with the plate of burekas... after all, you have to do something to offset all the health benefits.

# INGREDIENTS

(Serves 4-6)

1 cup fine bulgur
1 large head of lettuce
4-5 cups parsley
2 cups spring onion,
    only the green stem
1 cup fresh spearmint
¼ cup olive oil
Juice from 2 large lemons
Salt

# PREPARATION

Soak the bulgur for 15 minutes in 2 cups of pre-boiled water, until it absorbs the liquid.
Chop the lettuce, parsley, onion and spearmint as fine as you can. Save the spearmint for last, so it doesn't blacken.
In a wide bowl, mix the chopped vegetables with the olive oil and lemon juice, add the bulgur and continue mixing. Add the salt, mix, taste and adjust seasoning. Don't skimp on the lemon - tabule is meant to be sour!

## المقادير

(لـ 4-6 وجبات)

1 كوب برغل ناعم
1 خسة كبيرة
4-5 كوب بقدونس مفروم
2 كوب بصل أخضر مفروم
(بدون القسم الأبيض)
1 كوب نعنع مفروم
¼ كوب زيت زيتون
عصير 2 حبة ليمونة كبيرة
ملح حسب الرغبة

## طريقة التحضير

يُنقَع البرغل في 2 كوب من الماء المغلي لمدة ربع ساعة، حتى يتم امتصاص الماء. تُفرَم الخسة ويُضاف اليها البقدونس والبصل الأخضر والنعنع المفروم، ثم زيت الزيتون، البرغل، عصير الليمون والملح وتُخلَط المقادير جيّدًا.
(يُفرَم النعنع في النهاية حتى لا يسودّ لونه).

Fill crunchy lettuce leaves with tabule salad.
You can also garnish with pomegranate seeds or even edible flowers.

SERVING SUGGESTION

تُقدَّم التبولة على أوراق الخسّ. ويمكن تزيين التبولة بحبوب الرمان أو بالزهور القابلة للأكل.

# INGREDIENTS

(Serves 6)

1 cup red rice
1 teaspoon nutmeg
Salt and pepper
3 large potatoes, preferably long
5½ cups vegetable stock
    (see recipe on page 161)
1 cup concentrated tomato paste
1 teaspoon hot paprika
¼ cup chopped parsley
    or coriander

# PREPARATION

Soak the rice in boiling water for 30 minutes. Strain, move to a pot with 2½ cups vegetable stock and the nutmeg, salt and pepper. Cook for 30 minutes over medium heat. Cover the pot with a clean towel and let rest for 15 minutes.
Wash the potatoes well. In a pot, cover them (without peeling) in water, add ½ teaspoon of salt, and cook them over medium heat for 30-40 minutes. Make sure that they remain intact. Cool well.
Add the tomato paste to the remaining 3 cups of vegetable stock and bring to a boil. Season with hot paprika, salt and pepper and cook for 20 minutes over medium heat.
Carefully half the potatoes lengthwise, and using a small teaspoon make a 2 cm (4/5 inches) hole in each halve. Stuff with red rice and serve two halves to each person in a deep plate. Pour the tomato sauce on top and garnish with parsley or coriander.

UPGRADE

For a crunchy texture and a deeper flavor, you can deep-fry the potatoes after cooking, or bake them for 15 minutes in an oven preheated to 180 degrees C (350 degrees F).

# المقادير

(لـ 6 وجبات)

1 كوب أرز أحمر
1 ملعقة صغيرة جوزة الطيب
ملح وفلفل حسب الرغبة
3 حبات بطاطا كبيرة
    (مفضّل طويلة الشكل)
5½ كوب مرق خضار
    (الوصفة صفحة 161)
1 كوب معجون البندورة
1 ملعقة صغيرة ببريكا حارة
¼ كوب بقدونس/كزبرة مفروم/ة

# طريقة التحضير

يُنقَع الأرز في الماء المغلي لمدة نصف ساعة، ثم يُصفّى ويُطهى في قدر مع كوبين ونصف من مرق الخضار مع جوزة الطيب والملح والفلفل لمدة نصف ساعة على نار متوسطة. تُغطّى القدر بفوطة مطبخ نظيفة وتُترَك جانبًا لمدة ربع ساعة.
تُغسَل حبات البطاطا جيدا دون تقشيرها، وتُسلَق في الماء مع نصف ملعقة ملح لمدة 30-40 دقيقة على نار متوسطة، مع مراعاة عدم تفتّها. تُخرَج من الماء وتُترَك جانبًا حتى تبرد.
يُغلى 3 كوب من مرق الخضار المتبقي مع معجون البندورة، ويُضاف إليه الملح والفلفل الأسود والببريكا الحارة، ويُترَك ليغلي لمدة 20 دقيقة على نار متوسطة حتى يتماسك.
تُقطّع حبات البطاطا بالطول بحذر، وبواسطة ملعقة تُحفَر أنصاف البطاطا حتى عمق 2 سم تقريبًا، ثم تُحشى بالأرز الأحمر المطبوخ.
يُقدَّم في كل صحن نصفان من البطاطا ويُسكَب عليهما المرق وحفنة من البقدونس أو الكزبرة المفروم/ة.

طريقة أخرى

لتحسين المذاق، يمكن قلي البطاطا بعد سلقها، أو طهوها بفرن مسخّن مسبقا لحرارة 180 درجة، لمدة ربع ساعة.

# BATATA MA' ARUZ AHMAR POTATOES STUFFED WITH RED RICE

البطاطا مع الأرز الأحمر

Sometimes you have to embrace simple recipes. Especially when you're hungry and looking for a quick solution with simple ingredients you already have in the house. Potato 'boats' stuffed with red rice and swimming in a quick and easy tomato sauce is exactly that. The ingredients are modest and the result impressive. What more do you need, except for a carbohydrate craving?

# INGREDIENTS

(Serves 4-6)

## DOUGH

2 cups flour
½ cup water
⅓ cup oil
¼ teaspoon turmeric
1 teaspoon salt

## FILLING

2 cups chopped spinach
½ chopped onion, raw or fried
1 teaspoon sumac
½ small lemon
Salt

## COATING

1 tablespoon olive oil
1 tablespoon nigella or sesame seeds

# PREPARATION

## FOR THE DOUGH

Preheat oven to 180 degrees C (350 degrees F).
In a bowl, mix all of the ingredients until the
dough is uniform. Cover with shrink wrap and
refrigerate for 30 minutes.

## FOR THE FILLING

Wash the chopped spinach and dry well. In a
bowl, mix the spinach with the onion (if you fried
the onion, let it cool before adding) and stir in the
sumac, lemon and salt.
Divide the dough into six equal balls and, with a
rolling pin, roll them out to circles about 2 cm (1
inch) thick and 10 cm (4 inch) in diameter. Put a
spoonful of the filling at the center of each circle.
To make a triangle, fold the side closest to you
about a quarter of the way up. Form a diagonal
by folding the top right of the circle towards
the bottom left, to where it meets the first
fold. Close the left-hand side to complete the
triangle. Put the triangles in a baking dish lined
with parchment paper, brush with olive oil and
sprinkle with nigella or sesame seeds. Bake for
20 minutes, until the triangles are brown-golden.
Serve hot, preferably with salad or vegan yoghurt
(see recipe on page 162).

المقادير

(لـ 6 أقراص)

للعجين

2 كوب طحين
½ كوب ماء
⅓ كوب زيت
¼ ملعقة صغيرة كركم
1 ملعقة صغيرة ملح

للحشوة

2 كوب سبانخ مفروم
½ كوب بصل مفروم (نيء أو مقلي)
1 ملعقة صغيرة سماق
عصير نصف ليمونة صغيرة

للتزيين

1 ملعقة كبيرة زيت زيتون
1 ملعقة كبيرة قزحة أو سمسم

طريقة التحضير

العجين

تُخلَط كل مكوّنات العجينة في وعاء وتُعجَن حتى الحصول على
عجينة متجانسة ومتماسكة. تُغلَّف بالنايلون وتُترَك في الثلاجة لمدة
نصف ساعة.

الحشوة

يُغسَل السبانخ المفروم جيّدًا ويُصفَّى من الماء. يوضع السبانخ في
وعاء مع البصل (إذا اخترنا البصل المقلي فيُضاف بعد أن يبرد)، ثم
يُضاف السماق وعصير الليمون والملح.
يُقطَّع العجين إلى ست قطع متساوية، ثم تُرقّ كل قطعة على شكل
دائرة. نضع مقدار ملعقة كبيرة من الحشوة في منتصف كل دائرة
ونطويها على شكل مثلث بهذه الطريقة: نطوي القسم السفلي باتجاه
مركز الدائرة، ثم نطوي القسم الأيمن وأخيرا القسم الأيسر إلى نفس
النقطة، حتى نحصل على شكل مثلث.
توضَع الأقراص في صينية مغطاة بورق الخبز، ثمَّ تُدهن بزيت
الزيتون ويُرَشّ عليها السمسم أو القزحة. تُخبز في فرن مسخّن مسبقًا
على حرارة 180 درجة لمدة 20 دقيقة، حتى تصبح ذهبية اللون.
التقديم: تُقدَّم الأقراص ساخنة بجانب اللبن النباتي (الوصفة
صفحة 162) أو السلطة.

# AQRAS SABANEKH
## TRIANGLE SPINACH PASTRIES
### أقراص السبانخ

There are a lot of aqras variants in the Arab cuisine, some vegan and some not. What they all have in common is that they are stuffed pastries. The rest is left to interpretation and personal taste, and the sky – or the ingredients you happen to have in the refrigerator – is the limit. You can change the shape of the pastry (triangle, circle, square, or any shape you like) or the filling. Try this quick, turmeric scented dough with sour spinach filling to wake up any regular breakfast or sleepy brunch, and add your own variations. Walnuts, pine nuts, almonds or vegan cheese will be warmly accepted here.

# AQRAS AL-FITR MUSHROOM PASTRIES
## أقراص الفطر

Aqras al-fitr, one of the most common starters in the Arab cuisine, is a kind of large burek made from simple dough. You can stuff them with your favorite vegetables. Just make sure to double the recipe in advance, because they get snatched....

If you want to give the filling a rich, cheese-like taste, don't forget the nutritional yeast (not to be confused with baking yeast, remember!) which you can find in most natural food stores.

# INGREDIENTS

(Makes 6 units)

DOUGH

2 cups flour
½ cup water
⅓ cup oil
¼ teaspoon turmeric
1 teaspoon salt

FILLING

1 tablespoon oil
1 medium onion, diced
1 small red pepper, diced
1 cup forest mushrooms, diced
¼ cup nutritional yeast
Salt and pepper

# PREPARATION

FOR THE DOUGH

Preheat oven to 180 degrees C (350 degrees F). In a bowl, mix all of the ingredients until uniform and shape into a ball. Cover with shrink wrap and refrigerate for 30 minutes.

FOR THE FILLING

Heat the oil in a pan and fry the onion until golden. Add the red pepper, cover the pan and cook over low heat for 5 minutes.
Add the mushrooms and nutritional yeast to the pan, then salt and pepper to taste. Fry over medium heat for 10-15 minutes, stirring occasionally. Let cool to room temperature.

FOR THE FILLING

Take the dough out of the refrigerator, divide it into 6 balls and, using a rolling pin, roll them out to circles 2 cm (4/5 inches) thick and 10 cm (4 inch) in diameter. Put a spoonful of the filling in the center of each circle, fold in half and pinch the edge with your fingers, making sure it is completely sealed. Press the edge tight with the tines of a fork and make sure the filling is distributed evenly inside the dough. Arrange in a baking dish lined with parchment paper and bake for 15-20 minutes, until brown on the outside. Serve as a first course or as a side dish with the main course.

المقادير

(لـ 6 أقراص)

للعجين

2 كوب طحين
½ كوب ماء
⅓ كوب زيت
¼ ملعقة صغيرة كركم
1 ملعقة صغيرة ملح

للحشوة

1 ملعقة كبيرة زيت زيتون
1 بصلة متوسطة مقطّعة لمكعبات
1 فلفل أحمر حلو مقطّع لمكعبات
1 كوب فطر المحاري مقطّع لمكعبات
¼ كوب خميرة البيرة*
ملح وفلفل أسود حسب الرغبة

*خميرة البيرة هي بهار يعطي نكهة الجبنة بالوجبات الخضريّة ويمكن العثور عليه في محلّات المنتجات الخضرية. بالرغم من انّ الاسم يذكرنا باسم الخميرة العادية، لكن لا علاقة بينهما البتّة.

طريقة التحضير

العجينة

تُخلَط كل مكوّنات العجينة في وعاء وتُعجَن حتى الحصول على عجينة متجانسة ومتماسكة. تُغلَّف بالنايلون وتُترَك في الثلاجة لمدة نصف ساعة.

الحشوة

يُقلى البصل بالزيت حتى يصبح ذهبيّ اللون. يُضاف الفلفل الأحمر المقطّع وتُغطّى المقلاة وتُترك على نار هادئة لمدة 5 دقائق. يُضاف الفطر المقطّع وخميرة البيرة ويُنثر القليل من الملح والفلفل الأسود حسب الرغبة. يُترك الخليط على نار هادئة لمدة 10-15 دقيقة، ويُحرَّك كل بضعة دقائق حتى ينضج، ثمّ يُترَك جانبًا ليبرد.

تحضير الأقراص

يُقطَّع العجين إلى ست قطع متساوية، ويُرقّ كل منها على شكل دائرة. نضع ملعقة كبيرة من الحشوة في وسط كل دائرة ونطوي أطرافها لنحصل على شكل نصف دائري (راعوا عدم حدوث ثقوب في العجينة). نضغط على الأطراف بواسطة شوكة. تُوضع الأقراص في صينية مغطاة بورق الخبز، ثم تُخبَز في فرن مسخّن مسبقًا على حرارة 180 درجة لمدة 15-20 دقيقة، حتى تصبح ذهبيّة اللون. تُقدَّم كوجبة أولى أو كإضافة للوجبة الرئيسية.

# INGREDIENTS

(Serves 2-4)

3 colorful peppers – green, red and yellow
1 eggplant
1 potato
1 zucchini
¼ cup olive oil
¼ teaspoon sweet paprika
Salt and pepper

TOASTED PITA

1 pita
1 tablespoon olive oil

SERVING

1 sliced tomato
1 sliced cucumber
¼ cup tahini sauce
1 tablespoon cooked chickpeas
1 tablespoon sunflower or other seeds

# PREPARATION

Preheat the oven to 200 degrees C (400 degrees F). Cut all the vegetables into slices or strips and put in a glass dish. Pour the olive oil on the vegetables, season with paprika, salt and pepper and mix well. Bake the vegetables for 30-40 minutes, until the potatoes are ready. Remove from the oven and lower the temperature to 180 degrees C (350 degrees F).

FOR ROASTED PITA

Cut the pita into squares or strips and mix with the olive oil. Roast for 10 minutes, until golden.

FOR SERVING

Arrange the baked vegetables on a serving plate. Lay tomato and cucumber slices and the roasted pita over them, and pour tahini sauce on top of everything. Sprinkle the chickpeas and sunflower seeds on top and serve immediately.

UPGRADE

To vary the baked vegetables, add dry herbs (sage, thyme, oregano and rosemary) and exchange sumac for the paprika (which gives a slightly more sour taste and reddish color). You can also season the pita with za'atar and grated garlic along with the olive oil. To serve, you can also prepare green tahini or add fresh herbs, roasted pine nuts and lemon.

# المقادير

(لـ 2-4 وجبات)

3 حبات فلفل أخضر، أحمر وأصفر
1 حبة باذنجان
1 حبة بطاطا
1 حبة كوسا
¼ كوب زيت زيتون
¼ ملعقة صغيرة ببريكا حلوة
ملح وفلفل أسود حسب الرغبة

للخبز المقلي

رغيف خبز
1 ملعقة كبيرة زيت زيتون

للتقديم

1 حبة بندورة مقطعة
1 حبة خيارة مقطعة
¼ كوب صلصة طحينة
1 ملعقة حمص حب مسلوق
1 ملعقة كبيرة بذور عباد الشمس
او بذور اخرى

# طريقة التحضير

تُغسل الخضار وتُقطَّع حسب الرغبة، وتُوضَع في صينية فرن مغطّاة بورق الخبز. تُمزج البهارات بالزيت في وعاء، وتُدهن بها الخضار جيّدًا، ثم تُدخَل الصينية إلى فرن مسخَّن مسبقًا لحرارة 200 درجة، لمدة 30-40 دقيقة حتى تنضج الخضار. بعد إخراج الصينية تُخفَّف درجة حرارة الفرن الى 180 درجة.

الخبز المحمّص

يُقطَّع الرغيف إلى مكعبات. تُخلط مكعبات الخبز بالزيت وتُوضَع في صينية مغطّاة بورق الخبز، تُدخَل إلى الفرن لمدة عشر دقائق حتى تصبح ذهبيّة اللون.

التقديم

تُوضَع الخضار المشوية في قاع طبق عميق، وتُوضَع فوقها الخضار الطازجة (الخيار والبندورة)، ثم مكعبات الخبز المقرمشة. تُسكَب صلصة الطحينة فوق السلطة وتُنثَر عليها بذور عباد الشمس وحبوب الحمص.

للتنويع

من الممكن استخدام أنواع مختلفة من الخضروات، وإضافة الأعشاب الجافة واستبدال البريكا بالسُماق. كما يمكن إضافة الزعتر للخبز المحمّص والثوم المهروس.

# FATET AL-MAQALI VEGETABLES WITH TAHINI AND ROASTED PITA-BREAD
## فتة المقالي

This salad of both raw and roasted vegetables with oven-toasted pita-bread, tahini and warm chickpeas is an economic and colorful solution to enliven leftover bits of stale pitas. You're invited to improvise and add variations as your imagination sees fit.

**Tahini Sauce:** Combine ½ cup tahini, ¼ cup cold water, juice from ½ lemon and a teaspoon of salt, and mix until uniform. You can add water or tahini, depending on how thick you want the sauce, or spices and herbs for variety and color.

Before baking the eggplant I recommend that you sprinkle salt over the slices and leave them on a paper towel for 15 minutes to extract some of the liquids and bitterness.

TIP!

للتقليل من مرارة الباذنجان. يُفضَّل تقطيعه قبل الخبز. ورشَ الملح عليه من الجهتين وتركه حتى يفرز سوائله. ثم تجفيفه بورق المطبخ وخبزه حسب التعليمات.

Tel Aviv تل أبيب

# SINYET AL-KHUDAR MA' SEITAN
## SEITAN EGGROLL

صينية الخضار مع بروتين القمح

During my midterms I would do everything, but study. Cooking was my favorite mode of procrastination, and so I found myself experimenting in my small Tel Aviv kitchen. At times I really strayed away from my origins, more than once as all the way to the Asian cuisine. That was how I found myself rolling rice paper with familiar seasonings from home. As time went by I became vegan and finished my studies, but I still learn new things.

# INGREDIENTS

(Serves 4)

4 slices (400 grams, 1 pound)
   of seitan, homemade
   (see recipe on page 158) or store-bought
4 sheets of rice paper

### MARINADE

½ cup soy sauce
½ cup smokey barbecue
sauce
1 tablespoon hot paprika
1 tablespoon sweet paprika

### COATING

½ cup flour
¼ cup spicy chili sauce
1 cup tempura mix
Oil

# PREPARATION

### FOR THE SEITAN AND MARINADE

Mix all of the marinade ingredients in a wide bowl. Put the seitan slices in the bowl so they're submerged in the marinade. Cover with shrink wrap and refrigerate for at least 3 hours, or overnight, so they can absorb the flavors.

### ROLLING THE RICE PAPER

Soak the rice paper in tepid water for 2 minutes or until soft, and spread them out carefully on the work surface. Put a slice of seitan at the lower end of each sheet. Roll the sheet with the seitan upwards, almost until the end. Fold the two sides inward like an envelope and finish rolling. In the same manner, prepare all 4 rolls.

### FOR THE COATING

Prepare two plates. In one, mix the flour with ½ cup water and spicy chili sauce, and in the other, pour the tempura.
Dip the rolls in the first plate, and then the second. For a crispy coat – repeat the action: dip in the first plate again, and then in the second one.
In a pot, heat the oil and carefully deep-fry the rolls. Move to a paper towel.
Serve hot with oven-roasted vegetables or fresh salad.

### BONUS RECIPE

Try preparing this easy roasted vegetable side dish. Preheat the oven to 200 degrees C (400 degrees F). In a glass baking dish arrange 3 sliced peppers, 2 sliced potatoes and 1 sliced onion. Pour ⅓ cup olive oil on top and season with salt, sweet paprika, crushed or dried garlic and ½ tablespoon mustard (optional). You can also add the seitan marinade. Cover with foil and bake for 40 minutes, or until the potatoes are soft.

To more easily handle the rice paper, work over a clean towel.

TIP!

يمكن الاستعانة بفوطة نظيفة للفّ أوراق الأرز
عليها لتسهيل العملية.

## المقادير

(لـ 4 وجبات)

4 قطع بروتين القمح سواء من صنع بيتي
(الوصفة صفحة 158)
أو جاهز بالنكهة الطبيعية
4 لفائف ورق الأرز

### للتتبيلة

½ كوب صلصة الصويا
½ كوب باربيكيو مدخّن
1 ملعقة كبيرة ببريكا حارة
1 ملعقة كبير ببريكا حلوة

### للتغطية

½ كوب طحين
¼ كوب صلصة تشيلي حار
1 كوب خلطة التامبورا
زيت للقلي العميق

## طريقة التحضير

### بروتين القمح

تُخلَط كل مكوّنات التتبيلة في وعاء وتُنقَع فيها قطع بروتين القمح ثم تُغلَّف بالنايلون، وتُترَك في الثلاجة لمدة ليلة كاملة أو ثلاث ساعات على الأقل.

### لف أوراق الأرز

توضَع أوراق الأرز بالماء المغلي في وعاء لمدة 15 ثانية. أو حتى تطرى، ثمّ توضَع بحذر على طاولة العمل. تُفرَد كل ورقة وتوضَع في طرفها السفلي قطعة من بروتين القمح وتُلفّ إلى الأعلى ثم تُطوَى من الجانبين ويُضغط على الأطراف برفق حتى تلتصق. نكرر العملية مع باقي أوراق الأرز وقطع بروتين القمح.

### للتغليف

يُخلَط الطحين مع نصف كوب من الماء وصلصة التشيلي الحارة في وعاء واحد، وفي وعاء آخر تُوضَع خلطة التامبورا.
تُغمَس لفائف الأرز في وعاء الطحين أوّلاً ثم في وعاء التامبورا، ويتم تكرار العملية للحصول على قطع مقرمشة في القلي.
تُقلى لفائف الأرز بحذر في زيت عميق ساخن حتى تصبح ذهبيّة اللون، وتُصفّى بواسطة ورق المطبخ.
تُقدَّم ساخنة مع الخضار المشويّة بالفرن (أنظروا الوصفة فيما يلي) أو مع السلطة الطازجة.

### صينية الخضار بالفرن

تُقطَّع 3 حبات فلفل حلو بألوان مختلفة، 2 حبة بطاطا وبصلة واحدة إلى شرائح، وتُوضَع في صينية بايركس. يُوزَّع على الخضار ثلث كوب زيت زيتون ويُنثَر عليها الملح والببريكا الحلوة، ويضاف الثوم المهروس (الكمية حسب الرغبة) ونصف ملعقة كبيرة من الخردل (غير إلزامي). كما يمكن إضافة القليل من تتبيلة بروتين القمح.
تُغلَّف الصينية بقطعة من ورق الألومنيوم وتُوضَع في فرن مسخَّن مسبقًا على حرارة 200 درجة، لمدة 40 دقيقة أو حتى تنضج البطاطا.

# QARNABIT AND DUCHUN
## CAULIFLOWER AND MILLET

القرنبيط مع الدُّخن

A simple, improvised recipe you can prepare from the modest, everyday ingredients you have on hand, assuming you keep millet in your pantry. If you don't, here's your chance to start – millet is filling, healthy and goes wonderfully with sauces. The cauliflower can be baked or deep-fried in oil. That choice is, of course, a matter of health and taste.

# INGREDIENTS

(Serves 4)

CAULIFLOWER

1 medium cauliflower,
   broken into individual florets
1 tablespoon olive oil

TOMATO SAUCE

½ cup tomato paste
3 cups vegetable stock
   (see ingredient on page 161)
1 cup dried oregano
1 cup dried basil
Salt and pepper

MILLET

1 cup millet
2 cups vegetable stock
   (see recipe on page 161)
½ tablespoon cumin
Salt

MILLET

1 cup millet
2 cups vegetable stock
   (see recipe on page 161)
½ tablespoon cumin
Salt

# PREPARATION

FOR THE CAULIFLOWER

Preheat the oven to 200 degrees C (400 degrees F).
Arrange the florets on a baking dish lined with
parchment paper and brush with olive oil.
Bake for 20 minutes, until it's slightly (but not
completely) soft.

FOR THE TOMATO SAUCE

In a pot, bring all of the ingredients to a boil. Lower
the heat and cook for 20 minutes. Adjust seasoning
to taste.

FOR THE MILLET (PREPARED AT THE SAME TIME AS THE SAUCE)

Wash the millet well and strain. Put into a pot, add
the vegetable stock, season with cumin and salt and
bring to a boil. Lower the heat and simmer for 15-20
minutes, until all the water evaporates. Remove from
the stove, cover with a clean towel and the lid and
let rest for five minutes.

FOR SERVING

Serve the millet on a plate, with the cauliflower
arranged on top and  the tomato sauce over
everything. Best served with tahini sauce or vegan
yoghurt (see recipe on page 162).

### القرنبيط

تُوضَع زهرات القرنبيط في صينية فرن مغلّفة بورق الخبز وتُدهن الزهرات بزيت الزيتون، ثم تُدخَل إلى فرن مسخَّن مسبقًا على حرارة 200 درجة لمدة 20 دقيقة حتى تصبح ناضجة جزئيًا.

### للقرنبيط

1 قرنبيط متوسّط مقطّع لزهرات
1 ملعقة كبيرة زيت زيتون

### صلصة البندورة

تُسخَّن جميع مكوّنات الصلصة في قدر وتُترَك على النار لتغلي، ثم تُخفَّف الحرارة وتُطهى لمدة 20 دقيقة أخرى. يمكن تعديل المذاق بإضافة التوابل حسب الحاجة.

### لصلصة البندورة

½ كوب معجون البندورة
3 كوب مرق خضار
(الوصفة صفحة 161)
1 ملعقة كبيرة اوريجانو مجفف
1 ملعقة كبيرة ريحان مجفف
ملح وفلفل أسود حسب الرغبة

### الدخن (يُحضَّر في نفس الوقت مع الصلصة):

يُغسَل الدخن جيّدًا ويُصفّى من الماء، ثمّ يُوضَع في قدر ويُضاف إليه المرق والملح والكمون، ويُترَك على النار حتى يغلي. تُخفَّف الحرارة ويُطهى لمدة 15-20 دقيقة على نار هادئة حتى تجفّ السوائل. بعد أن ينضج تُوضَع فوطة مطبخ نظيفة على القدر، وتُترَك القدر جانبًا لمدة 5 دقائق.

### الدُّخن

1 كوب دخن
2 كوب مرق خضار
(الوصفة صفحة 161)
½ ملعقة كبيرة كمون
ملح حسب الرغبة

### التقديم

يُوضَع الدخن في طبق التقديم وعليه زهرات القرنبيط وتُسكَب فوقه صلصة البندورة. يُقدَّم بجانب صلصة الطحينة أو اللبن النباتي. (انظروا الوصفة صفحة 162).

**Variation:** For a crunchy texture, you can deep-fry the cauliflower instead of baking.

للتنويع: يمكن قلي القرنبيط في زيت عميق وساخن بدلا من خبزه في الفرن.

# INGREDIENTS

(Serves 4-6)

2 cups small, dried fava beans
½ cup dried soy beans
1 teaspoon baking powder
¼ cup bush okra, chopped
¼ cup coriander or parsley, chopped
Juice from 1 large lemon
½ teaspoon salt
½ teaspoon cumin

FRIED ONION

1 large onion, halved and sliced
1 cup tempura mix
Frying oil

# PREPARATION

FOR THE DIP

In separate large pots, cover the fava and soy beans with water and soak overnight. Strain, cover the fava beans with fresh water, add the baking powder (to make the cooking quicker), and boil for about an hour over medium heat, until they are soft. Saving a ½ cup of the cooking water, strain, cool and peel the fava beans – make sure to discard the skins for a smooth texture.
At the same time, cook the soy beans in another pot with a lot of water for an hour over medium heat, until soft.
In a food processor, blend the skinned fava beans, soy beans, coriander (or parsley), bush okra, lemon juice, fava bean cooking water and spices to a smooth paste. Taste and adjust seasoning.

FOR THE FRIED ONION

Separate the onion into strips and coat well in tempura.
In a wide pan, heat the oil (about 4 tablespoons) and fry the onion strips.
Pour the paste into individual serving bowls, garnish with the fried onion strips and serve.

المقادير

(لـ 4-6 وجبات)

2 كوب فول يابس صغير الحبة
½ كوب فول الصويا
1 ملعقة كبيرة باكينج باودر
¼ كوب ملوخية ناشفة أو خضراء مفرومة
¼ كوب كزبرة/بقدونس مفرومة/مفروم
عصير ليمونة كبيرة
½ ملعقة صغيرة ملح
½ ملعقة صغيرة كمون
½ كوب من ماء سلق الفول

للبصل المقلي

1 بصلة كبيرة مقطعة لأنصاف دوائر
1 ملعقة كبيرة من خليط التامبورا
زيت للقلي

طريقة التحضير

يُنقَع الفول في وعاء كبير لمدة ليلة كاملة، ثم يُصفّى ويُغمر بماء نظيف (2 لتر) ويُطهَى مع الباكينج باودر (تساعد في عملية النضج) لمدة ساعة على نار متوسطة، حتى ينضج الفول تمامًا. بعد تبريده من الضروري تقشير الفول للحصول على هريس متجانس.
في أثناء طهي الفول، يُسلَق فول الصويا في قدر أخرى على نار متوسطة لمدة ساعة حتى ينضج تمامًا.
تُضاف الملوخية والكزبرة (أو البقدونس) للخلاط الكهربائي مع الفول وفول الصويا المسلوق وعصير الليمون والبهارات، وتُطحَن حتى الحصول على هريس متجانس. يمكن تعديل المذاق بإضافة التوابل حسب الحاجة.

البصل المقلي

تُفصَّل شرائح البصل المقطّعة عن بعضها، وتُغمَس في التامبورا حتى تغطيها جيّدًا، ثم تُقلى في 4 ملاعق كبيرة من الزيت في مقلاة ساخنة.
تُسكَب البيصارة في صحون التقديم الشخصية، وتُزيَّن بشرائح البصل المقلية.

# BISARA FAVA BEAN AND HERB DIP | البيصارة

Fava and soy beans make this Egyptian side-dish very high in protein and other nutrients. It can be used as a spread, but is most fun when served in personal bowls with a heap of crunchy, fried onion on top, and pitas for dipping, to offset some of the health benefits...

# MUTABAL EGGPLANT-TAHINI SPREAD | المتبّل / الباذنجان بالطحينة

Who doesn't like eggplant? Or tahini? Eggplant, in all its various forms, is a staple of the Arab cuisine, and a real meze lunch isn't complete without it, tahini, or both. Tahini is a perfect partner for eggplant – it's vegan, it's healthy and they go together like hummus and pita... this easy salad is great as a first course, a meze or a spread for sandwiches.

# INGREDIENTS

(Serves 4)

2 medium eggplants, preferably seedless
  (better for a smooth texture)
½ cup tahini
Juice from ½ large lemon
2 garlic cloves
2 tablespoon olive oil
¼ cup cold water
Salt

# PREPARATION

Preheat the oven to 200 degrees C (400 degrees F).
Wash the eggplants and, using the tip of a knife,
make several holes in each.
Line a baking dish with parchment paper, arrange
the eggplants on it and roast for 15-20 minutes,
until soft.
Cut each eggplant lengthwise and singe over a
high flame. You can - and are encouraged to -
put them directly on the fire. Let the eggplants
cool and carefully remove the skin. Remove any
seeds too, as much as possible.
Put the skinned eggplants, along with the rest of
the ingredients, in a food processor, and blend
until uniform. Adjust seasoning to taste. Serve
with hot pitas and pickles.

# المقادير

(لـ 4 وجبات)

2 حبة باذنجان متوسط الحجم
½ كوب طحينة
عصير نصف ليمونة كبيرة
2 فص ثوم
2 ملعقة كبيرة زيت زيتون
¼ كوب ماء بارد
ملح حسب الرغبة

# طريقة التحضير

يُفضَّل اختيار الباذنجان القليل البذور (لقوام أفضل). يُغسل
الباذنجان ويُجفَّف، ثم يُثقَب بواسطة سكين عدة مرات، ويوُضَع في
صينية مغطاة بورق الخبز في فرن مسخَّن مسبقا لحرارة 200 درجة،
لمدة 15-20 دقيقة حتى يصبح طريًّا. يُقطَّع الباذنجان بالطول وتُشوى
قشرته على نار الغاز مباشرة.
بعد أن يبرد تُنتزَع القشرة والبذور إن وُجدت قدر الإمكان، ثم يُخلَط
الباذنجان في الخلاط الكهربائي مع الطحينة وعصير الليمون والثوم
والملح والماء حتى الحصول على قوام متجانس. يُقدم مع الخبز
الساخن والمخللات.

## SEITAN & MUSHROOM SHAWARMA
### شاورما بروتيد القمح مع الفطر

Ask the average Israeli what the favorite foods in Israel are, and you would probably find the same familiar friends at the top of the list: hummus, falafel and shawarma. Hummus and falafel are vegan since birth, but what about shawarma? Well, you don't have to give up on your love for shawarma, but you can definitely forego the suffering caused by meat production. This yummy vegan version even tastes like the original. The secret is to make the seitan yourself, and to get the seasoning right.

# INGREDIENTS

(Serves 4-6)

1 pack (250 g, about 0.55 lb)
  brown champignon mushrooms
1 pack (300 g, about 0.65 lb) seitan,
  homemade (see recipe on page 158)
  or store-bought
1 medium onion
¼ cup olive oil
1 teaspoon amba
1 tablespoon turmeric
Salt and pepper

# PREPARATION

Cut the mushrooms and seitan into strips. Halve and
slice the onion.
In a pan, heat the olive oil and fry the onion over
medium heat until golden. Add the mushroom strips,
the seitan, the amba and the spices, stir lightly
and cover. Cook over medium heat for 20 minutes,
stirring occasionally. Serve inside a pita or wrap with
tahini, vegetables and pickles, or on a serving plate.

# المقادير

(لـ 4-6 وجبات)

1 سلة (250 غرام) فطر شامبنيون
1 رزمة (300 غرام) من بروتين
القمح سواء من صنع بيتي
(الوصفة صفحة 158)
أو جاهز بالنكهة الطبيعية
1 بصلة متوسطة
¼ كوب زيت زيتون
1 ملعقة صغيرة عمبة
1 ملعقة كبيرة كركم
ملح وفلفل أسود حسب الرغبة

# طريقة التحضير

يُقطَّع الفقع إلى أنصاف وبروتين القمح لشرائح بالطول والبصل
لشرائح نصف دائرة. يُقلى البصل بالزيت على نار متوسطة حتى
يصبح ذهبيّ اللون. يُضاف الفقع، بروتين القمح، العمبة ثم البهارات
وتُحرّك. تُغطّى المقلاة وتُطهى محتوياتها على نار متوسطة لمدة 20
دقيقة مع مراعاة تحريكها من حين لآخر.
التقديم: تُقدَّم في رغيف خبز أو رغيف صاج مع إضافة صلصة
الطحينة وتشكيلة من الخضار والمخلّلات. ويمكن أيضًا تقديمها في
طبق.

Tahini Sauce: Combine ½ cup tahini, ¼ cup cold
water, juice from ½ lemon and a teaspoon of salt,
and mix until uniform. You can add water or tahini,
depending on how thick you want the sauce, or
spices and herbs for variety and color.

# BASCOT WO SIMSEM SESAME BISCUIT | البسكويت بالسمسم

The sesame biscuit is at once an easy cookie recipe to prepare with children, an excellent vegan snack to keep in your bag and a great addition to your morning coffee (or tea). And guess what? It only takes 30 minutes to prepare and doesn't require any special ingredients, except maybe coconut oil.

# INGREDIENTS

(Makes 10 units)

DOUGH

¾ cup (75 g) roasted sesame seeds
¼ cup brown sugar
½ cup coconut oil
1½ cups flour
1 tablespoon tahini
1 teaspoon dry yeast

GLAZING

¼ cup water
1 tablespoon sugar
¼ cup sesame seeds

# PREPARATION

Preheat the oven to 180 degrees C (350 degrees F).
In a bowl, combine all of the dough ingredients, until
you have a soft and uniform dough.
Form the dough into elongated 'fingers' and put
them on a baking dish lined with parchment paper.
Mix the sugar into the water and brush the fingers.
Sprinkle the sesame seeds on top.
Bake for 20 minutes, until the biscuits are golden.
Serve with spearmint tea or black coffee.

المقادير

(لـ 10 أقراص)

¾ كوب (75 غرامًا) سمسم
محمص
¼ كوب سكر بنّي
½ كوب زيت جوز الهند
1½ كوب طحين
1 ملعقة كبيرة طحينة
1 ملعقة صغيرة خميرة فورية

للتزيين

¼ كوب سمسم
¼ كوب ماء
1 ملعقة كبيرة سكر

طريقة التحضير

تُخلَط جميع المكوّنات (ما عدا السمسم للتزيين) في وعاء حتى
الحصول على عجينة متجانسة وطرية. تُقطَّع العجينة إلى كرات
وتُشكَّل منها دوائر صغيرة أو أصابع طويلة، تُدهن بخليط الماء مع
السكر ويُنثَر عليها السمسم للزينة. تُوضع في صينية فرن مغطاة بورق
الخبز، وتُخبَز في فرن مسخّن مسبقًا على حرارة 180 درجة لمدة 20
دقيقة حتى تصبح قطع البسكويت ذهبية اللون. يُقدَّم البسكويت مع
الشاي بالنعنع أو القهوة.

# INGREDIENTS

(Makes 10 units)

### DONUTS

2 cups flour
1 cup corn starch
1 tablespoon sugar
¼ teaspoon salt
1 tablespoon dry yeast
¼ teaspoon ground cardamom
2½ cups non-dairy milk,
    preferably unsweetened almond
1 teaspoon lemon juice
Deep-frying oil

### QATAR SYRUP

2 cups brown sugar
1 cup water
1 tablespoon lemon juice
1 tablespoon rose water

# PREPARATION

### FOR THE DONUTS

In a large bowl, combine all of the dry ingredients.
Gradually add the milk and lemon juice and carefully
knead until uniform and very soft. Cover with a towel
and leave in a warm place for 30 minutes.
In a pot, heat the oil until boiling. Make small balls
from the dough and carefully fry for 3-4 minutes,
until golden. Move to a dish covered with a paper
towel.

### FOR THE QATAR SYRUP
(PREFERABLY MADE IN ADVANCE AND HEATED BEFORE SERVING)

Cook the sugar and water over medium heat until
completely dissolved. Add the lemon and rose water
and stir until boiling. Lower the heat and cook for 15
more minutes. Pour over the hot donuts and serve.

# المقادير

(لـ 10 أقراص)

2 كوب طحين
1 ملعقة كبيرة نشاء
1 ملعقة كبيرة سكر
¼ ملعقة صغيرة ملح
1 ملعقة كبيرة خميرة فورية
¼ ملعقة صغيرة هيل مطحون
2½ كوب حليب نباتي
(مفضل حليب لوز غير محلّى)
1 ملعقة صغيرة عصير ليمون
زيت للقلي

### للقطر

2 كوب سكر بني
1 كوب ماء
1 ملعقة كبيرة عصير ليمون
1 ملعقة كبيرة ماء الزهر

# طريقة التحضير

### للعوامة

تُخلَط جميع المقادير الجافة، ويُضاف إليها تدريجيًّا الحليب والنشاء
وعصير الليمون، وتُدعَك جيّدًا حتى الحصول على عجينة متجانسة
ورخوة. تُغطَّى العجينة وتُترَك حتى تختمر في مكان دافئ لمدة نصف
ساعة.
نقتطع بمساعدة ملعقة صغيرة قطعًا صغيرة ونشكّلها على شكل
كرات، ثم تُقلى في زيت عميق وساخن جدًّا، لمدة 3-4 دقائق حتى
تصبح ذهبية اللون، ثم تصفّى من الزيت بواسطة ورق المطبخ.

### إعداد القطر (مفضل تحضيره مسبقًا وتسخينه قبل التقديم)

يُغلَى الماء والسكر على نار متوسطة حتى يذوب السكر، ثم يُضاف
عصير الليمون وماء الزهر ويُحرَّك القطر حتى يغلي. تُخفَّف النار
ويُترَك ليغلي على نار هادئة لمدة ربع ساعة. يُسكب القطر على العوامة
الساخنة وتُقدَّم.

# AWAME' DONUT HOLES

## العوامة (القمة القاضي)

Small, cardamom and rose water scented donuts originating from Lebanon. "'Awame" means "floating," and refers to that magical moment while frying when the donuts float to the top of the oil. They're also called "lokamet al-kadi" – "the judge's bite," to signify they were eaten by distinguished people.

# INGREDIENTS

(Makes a 16X22 cm [6X8½ inch] baking dish)

(المقادير لصينية فرن 22×16 سم)

### BOTTOM LAYER

1 cup fine semolina
3 cups non-dairy milk,
    preferably unsweetened almond
¼ cup sugar
2 tablespoon rose water
½ teaspoon vanilla extract
1 tablespoon corn starch

### TOP LAYER

2 cups non-dairy milk,
    preferably unsweetened almond
¼ cup vegan butter
¼ cup sugar
2 tablespoon cornstarch

### SERVING

½ cup crushed pistachios
½ cup crushed almonds
¼ cup rose water

## للطبقة الاولى

1 كوب سميد ناعم
3 كوب حليب نباتي
(مفضل حليب اللوز غير المحلّى)
¼ كوب سكر
2 ملعقة كبيرة ماء الزهر / الورد
½ ملعقة صغيرة فانيليا سائلة
1 ملعقة كبيرة نشاء

## للطبقة الثانية

2 كوب حليب نباتي
(مفضل حليب لوز غير محلّى)
¼ كوب زبدة نباتية
¼ كوب سكر
2 ملعقة كبيرة نشاء

## للتقديم

½ كوب فستق حلبي مطحون
½ كوب لوز مطحون
¼ كوب ماء زهر أو ماء ورد

# PREPARATION

### طريقة التحضير

### FOR THE BOTTOM LAYER

In a pot, heat the semolina, non-dairy milk, rose water and vanilla extract, and cook over medium heat for 15 minutes, stirring constantly to avoid lumps.
Dissolve the corn starch in a ¼ cup cold water, add to the pot and cook over low heat for 5 more minutes, stirring constantly. Pour the mixture into a dish and refrigerate for at least an hour, until solid.

### الطبقة الأولى

يُسخَّن السميد، الحليب، ماء الزهر، والفانيليا السائلة في قدر على نار متوسطة، مع التحريك الدائم حتى لا تلتصق المقادير، وذلك لمدة ربع ساعة تقريبا حتى تتبخّر السوائل.
يُذوَّب النشاء مع ربع كوب ماء، ويُضاف للقدر حتى يغلي على نار هادئة لمدة خمس دقائق مع مراعاة التحريك المستمر. يُسكب المزيج في صينية، وتُوضَع الصينية في الثلاجة لمدة ساعة واحدة على الأقل حتى يتماسك المزيج.

### FOR THE TOP LAYER

Heat the milk, vegan butter and sugar over low heat until melted. Dissolve the corn starch in ½ cup of cold water, add to the pot and cook over low heat for thirty minutes, stirring constantly, until the mixture is very thick.
Pour it over the bottom layer, and refrigerate at least overnight.

### الطبقة الثانية

يُسخَّن الحليب في قدر مع الزبدة النباتية والسكر على نار متوسطة حتى تذوب جميع المقادير.
يُذوَّب النشاء مع ربع كوب من الماء، ويُضاف للقدر حتى يغلي لمدة نصف ساعة مع التحريك المستمر. يُسكب المزيج على الطبقة الأولى، ويُوضع في الثلاجة ويُترك لمدة ليلة كاملة حتى يتماسك.

### FOR THE SERVING

Sprinkle with crushed almonds and pistachios and pour rose water on top. Serve cold.

### التقديم

تُقدَّم الحلوى باردة بعد أن يُنثَر عليها اللوز والفستق الحلبي وماء الزهر.

# LAYALI LUBNAN
## LEBANESE NIGHTS | ليالي لبنان

Lebanese Nights, also called Beirutian Nights, is a rose scented, Lebanese, two-layer desert. When I first made it for my family I didn't tell them it was vegan until after they ate it. You should have seen their faces when they found out!

Photography by Nimrod Dean Kuchel

# Prague

## براغ

### A Volcano of Energy
### بركان الطاقات

# Chapter Three

# Prague

براغ

As the plane left the runway and soared into the sky, so did my heart. After twenty-eight years in Israel, I needed a change of scenery. The political tension was wearing me down. The conflict between Jews and Arabs weighed on me. I felt I was wasting all my energy in useless directions. Instead of realizing my dreams I was stuck in endless discussions about politics and feminism. It wasn't the life I wanted.

It became clear that in order to maintain my sanity, I would have to break free and start working on the projects I dreamt of. Despite my great love for my family, our special bond, the support of all the many friends who had become part of my life, and my challenging and satisfying work as a geriatric occupational therapist, I took a big chance and moved to beautiful Prague.

I still remember landing at the airport and loading into the trunk of the cab the four suitcases that contained my entire life story. I held my head high and felt the adrenaline pump through my veins. I started to learn the language, acclimatize, integrate into the city and get used to its special smell.

After a year in this magical place, now my second home, I'm happy I left Israel. Here, at last, I have peace of mind. Life is less intense here, and I can look at my home country with a fresh perspective. I have the will and strength, now, to do everything in my power to make it more beautiful.

I admit, with regret, that I didn't have the power to realize my dreams when I lived in my own country. I had to learn over the years to listen to my body and soul and not to put too much on my plate – which already was quite full just living there. But no matter where my body lives, in my thoughts I'm always present in the land where I was born.

About a year and a half before I left Israel, I started posting publicly on social media. At first I wrote in both Hebrew and Arabic, but soon, for convenience, switched to only Hebrew. Soon I met people from all walks of life: Jews and Arabs, secular and religious, Ultra-orthodox and atheists, right-wing and left. Some of them have become personal friends and significant parts of my life.

This exposure, the privilege of an unmediated encounter with the full spectrum of Israeli society, enriched my identity. I explored and strengthened my ability to influence and be influenced, to accept the other and make myself accepted without any judgement, as an equal among equals. Amidst fierce arguments, I discovered special people. Thanks to the open door of social media, I could connect with all these diverse individuals, and all together, they helped realize my dream, the product of which you are holding in your hand.

In this chapter, I'm pleased to present to you my more elaborate dishes – vegan gourmet, if you like. But there's no need for labels. Any cook who enjoys a challenge will particularly enjoy this chapter, but the dishes would be a welcome upgrade to any festive dinner with your family, or gathering with your friends.

# MUSAKHAN RA'IF WITH VEGAN MINCE | المسخّن

Sukhan means "hot," and that's how this wonderful dish derives its name – it should be served as hot as possible. It's usually made up of ra'if, homemade pita, with plenty of well-seasoned pieces of chicken and roasted pine nuts. What you have here is the vegan version, which keeps the dish's traditional flavors, but adds spinach to the ra'if and replaces the chicken with vegan mince. Best served on a common tray and shared lovingly.

**Tahini Sauce:**
Combine ½ cup tahini, ¼ cup cold water, juice from ½ lemon and a teaspoon of salt, and mix until uniform. You can add water or tahini, depending on how thick you want the sauce, or spices and herbs for variety and color.

# INGREDIENTS

(Serves 6)

## DOUGH

3 cups fresh spinach, chopped
3 cups flour
1 teaspoon salt
1 tablespoon sugar
2 tablespoon olive oil
½ teaspoon baking soda

## VEGAN MINCE

1 cup olive oil
2 cups vegan mince, homemade
   (see recipe on page 160) or store-bought
1 teaspoon sweet paprika
1 teaspoon dried garlic powder
Salt and pepper
½ cup roasted pine nuts

# PREPARATION

## FOR THE DOUGH

Cook the spinach in ¼ cup boiling water over medium heat for 2 minutes, until wilted. Strain the water, transfer to a food processor and blend until smooth. In another bowl, combine the flour, salt, sugar and baking soda. Add the spinach, the olive oil and ¾ cup of water, and knead well. Add another ¼ cup of water and continue kneading until the dough is soft but not sticky – if the dough is too sticky, add a table spoon of flour (or more, as needed), and if it's too dry, add a tablespoon of water (or more). Cover with shrink wrap and refrigerate for 30 minutes. Take the dough out and divide it into 6 balls. Spread flour on a surface and roll out each ball to a 2 cm (4/5 inch) thick circle. Heat a non-stick pan and fry the circles (without oil!) for 3-5 minutes on each side, until brown spots appear. Keep warm.

## FOR THE VEGAN MINCE

In another pan, fry the onion in the olive oil until golden. Add the vegan mince and cook for 5 more minutes.

## FOR SERVING

Spoon a generous helping of the vegan mince on each pita, sprinkle with roasted pine nuts and serve warm. Best with cold, sour vegan yoghurt, (see recipe on page 162) or tahini sauce, and a chopped salad

# المقادير

(لـ 6 وجبات)

## للعجين

3 كوب سبانخ مغسول ومفروم
3 كوب طحين
1 ملعقة صغيرة ملح
1 ملعقة كبيرة سكر
2 ملعقة كبيرة زيت زيتون
½ ملعقة صغيرة بيكربونات الصودا

## لخلطة بروتين الصويا المطحون

3 بصل متوسط الحجم مقطع لمكعبات
1 كوب زيت زيتون
2 كوب من بروتين الصويا المطحون سواء من صنع بيتي (الوصفة صفحة 160) أو جاهز بالنكهة الطبيعية
1 ملعقة صغيرة ببريكا حلوة
1 ملعقة صغيرة بودرة الثوم
ملح وفلفل أسود حسب الرغبة
½ كوب صنوبر محمّص

# طريقة التحضير

## العجين

يُسلَق السبانخ مع ربع كوب من الماء المغلي على نار متوسطة لمدة دقيقتين، ثم يُصفّى من الماء ويُطحَن ناعمًا بالخلاط الكهربائي حتى الحصول على مزيج متجانس وأملس.
تُخلَط مكوّنات العجين الجافة في وعاء: الطحين والسكر والملح، ثم يُضاف السبانخ المطحون وزيت الزيتون مع ¾ كوب ماء وتُخلط المكوّنات جيّدًا. يُضاف ¼ كوب ماء وتُعجَن المكونات حتى الحصول على عجينة متجانسة وطرية ولكن غير دَبِقة. يمكن إضافة الماء حسب الحاجة للحصول على التركيبة المناسبة. تُوضع العجينة في الثلاجة لمدة نصف ساعة.
تُقطَّع العجينة إلى 6 كرات متساوية، وتُفرَد إلى دوائر كبيرة أو متوسطة الحجم (حسب حجم المقلاة) سُمكها 2 سم.
في مقلاة غير لاصقة ساخنة يُقلى (بدون زيت) كل رغيف لمدة 3-5 دقائق من كل جهة حتى تظهر عليها بقع بنيّة.

## خلطة بروتين الصويا المطحون

يُقلى البصل بزيت الزيتون حتى يذبل ويصبح ذهبيّ اللون، ثم يُضاف إليه بروتين الصويا المطحون والبهارات، ويُحرّك المزيج حتى ينضج.

## التقديم

تُوضع كمية لا بأس بها من الحشوة على كل رغيف، ويُزيَّن بالصنوبر المحمّص. تُقدَّم الوجبة ساخنة بجانب اللبن النباتي (الوصفة صفحة 162)، أو صلصة الطحينة وسلطة الخضار.

# INGREDIENTS

(Serves 4)

1 cup finely crushed Freekeh*
   (available in markets and spice-shops)
1 tablespoon olive oil
1 medium onion, finely diced
5 cups vegetable stock
   (see recipe on page 161)
1 teaspoon cumin
1 teaspoon white pepper
Salt and pepper
Lemon slices

# PREPARATION

Carefully pick through the Freekeh to remove any
small stones. Wash well and soak in hot water for 15
minutes. Move to a strainer and wash under the tap,
until the water runs clear. Strain the excess water.
Heat the olive oil in a deep pot and fry the onion
until brown, to give the soup a deeper flavor. Add
the Freekeh and mix for 2 minutes over high heat.
Add the vegetable stock and spices, stir well and
bring to a boil. Lower the heat to medium, cover and
let the soup cook for 40-45 more minutes, until the
Freekeh softens and the soup thickens. Stir every 15
minutes or so, to avoid the Freekeh sticking to the
bottom of the pot.
Serve hot, with slices of lemon. You can also garnish
with fresh red onion.

---

* If you can only find whole Freekeh,
blend a cup of it with hot water in a food processor. 5-6
pulses should be enough. You can also use a spice-grinder
if you have one, and then you don't need to add water.

## المقادير

(لـ 4 وجبات)

1 كوب فريكة ناعمة*
1 ملعقة كبيرة زيت زيتون
1 بصلة متوسطة مفرومة ناعمًا
5 كوب مرق خضار
(الوصفة صفحة 161)
ملح وفلفل أسود حسب الرغبة
1 ملعقة كبيرة كمون
1 ملعقة كبيرة فلفل أبيض
شرائح ليمون للتقديم

## طريقة التحضير

تُنقّى الفريكة من الشوائب، وتُغسل جيدا ثم تُنقع بالماء الساخن
لمدة ربع ساعة. تُغسل الفريكة مرة أخرى جيدا تحت مياه جارية حتى
يصفو الماء تماما وتُصفّى.
يُقلى البصل بزيت الزيتون في قدر كبيرة حتى يصبح لونه ذهبيًّا، ثم
تُضاف الفريكة وتُقلّب مع البصل لمدة دقيقتين على نار عالية.
يُضاف مرق الخضار والبهارات، وتُخلط المحتويات جيّدًا وتُترك لتغلي.
تُخفّف الحرارة وتُغطّى القدر وتُترك على نار هادئة لمدة 40-45 دقيقة
حتى تنضج الفريكة ويتماسك قوام الشوربة. من المهم تحريك
المحتويات من حين إلى آخر تفاديًا لالتصاقها.
تُقدّم الفريكة ساخنة مع شرائح الليمون، كما يمكن تزيين الطبق
بالبصل البنفسجي حسب الرغبة.

---

*إذا لم تتوفر لديكم فريكة ناعمة،
يمكنكم طحن حبوب الفريكة الكاملة
مع إضافة الماء الساخن خمس أو ست
مرات، أو دقّها جافة في الهاون المُعدّ
لطحن البهارات والحبوب.

# SHORBET AL-FREEKEH GREEN WHEAT SOUP | شوربة الفريكة

Freekeh is wheat that was harvested green - before it ripened. Roasting the grains gives the Freekeh an incomparable smoky aroma. It can be cooked like rice (see recipe on page 118), or, as in this recipe, into a soup. It is a warm, rich and filling dish, best suited for winter days. My mom used to serve this soup for special guests at festive dinners. To this day, the smell when I cook it reminds me of childhood and the first rain.

Prague براغ

| 117 |

# FREEKEH MUFALFALEH SMOKED GREEN WHEAT | الفريكة المفلفلة

You can cook Freekeh, roasted green wheat, as a soup (see recipe on page 116), or as in this recipe, like rice (Mufalfaleh, loosely translated, means fluffed rice). Don't neglect to rinse the Freekeh before cooking – that's the only way to get rid of the bitterness for a perfect dish. Serve as a festive side, or as a rich main course in its own right.

# INGREDIENTS

(Serves 4-6)

3 cups Freekeh, coarsely crushed
1 tablespoon olive oil
½ onion, diced
½ cup thin soup noodles (vermicelli)
6 cups vegetable stock
　(see recipe on page 161)
Salt and pepper

(see recipe on page 161)

SERVING

¼ cup roasted almonds

# PREPARATION

Pick well through the Freekeh to remove any small stones. Soak in boiling water for 15 minutes. Move the Freekeh to a strainer and wash well under the tap, until the water runs clear. Strain the excess fluid well.

In a deep pot, heat the olive oil and fry the onion until golden. Add the noodles and fry, stirring until they brown. Add the Freekeh and stir for 2 minutes over high heat.

Add the vegetable stock, season with salt and pepper and bring to a boil. Lower the heat, cover the pot and cook for 30 minutes, until all the liquid is absorbed. Remove from heat, cover with a clean towel and let the Freekeh rest for 15 minutes. Sprinkle with roasted almonds and serve hot. The Freekeh goes well with a fresh salad.

# المقادير

(لـ 4-6 وجبات)

3 كوب فريكة خشنة
1 ملعقة كبيرة زيت زيتون
½ بصلة متوسطة مقطعة لمكعبات
½ كوب شعيرية رقيقة للشوربة
6 كوب مرق خضار
(الوصفة صفحة 161)
ملح وفلفل أسود حسب الرغبة

للتقديم

¼ كوب لوز محمّص

# طريقة التحضير

تُنقّى الفريكة من الشوائب، وتُغسل جيدا ثم تُنقع بالماء الساخن لمدة ربع ساعة. تُغسل الفريكة مرة أخرى جيدا تحت مياه جارية حتى يصفو الماء تماما ثمّ تُصفّى.

يُقلى البصل بزيت الزيتون في قدر حتى يصبح ذهبيّ اللون. تُضاف الشعيرية للقدر، وتُقلّب حتى تصبح ذهبية اللون. تُضاف الفريكة وتُقلّب لمدة دقيقتين، ثمّ يُسكب مرق الخضار ويُنثر الملح والفلفل الأسود وتُترك القدر على النار حتى تغلي. تُخفّف الحرارة وتُغطّى القدر وتُترك على نار هادئة لمدة نصف ساعة حتى تتبخّر السوائل. بعد إزالتها عن النار، تُغطّى القدر بفوطة مطبخ نظيفة لمدة ربع ساعة. يُزيّن طبق الفريكة باللوز المحمّص، ويُقدّم ساخنًا بجانب السلطة.

# FASULYE WHITE BEANS & QUINOA

## الفاصولياء والكينوا

Fasulye is not a common ingredient in Arab cooking. This is one of maybe two dishes that feature it. It's easy to make, very nutritious and very popular, especially with children. The traditional dish is already vegan, so I didn't have to make any changes to the recipe. I left it alone, except for one small twist at the end – adding celery stalk.

# INGREDIENTS

(Serves 6)

FASULYE

2 cups dried white beans
1 tablespoon baking powder
4 tablespoon tomato paste
6 cups vegetable stock
    (see recipe on page 161)
3 celery stalks, diced
1 tablespoon dried basil
Salt and pepper

QUINOA

2 cups white quinoa
4 cups vegetable stock
    (see recipe on page 161)
Salt, white pepper, and black pepper

# PREPARATION

FOR THE FASULYE

Cover the beans with a lot of water and soak overnight (or for at least 8 hours). During summer, it's best to refrigerate them, but in winter, you can leave them out.
Strain the beans. Cook them in a large pot with 2 liters of water and the baking powder and cook for an hour, until partially soft.
Strain well, and return the beans to the pot. Add the tomato paste and vegetable stock and bring to a boil. Cover and cook for 15 minutes over low heat. Season to taste and cook covered for 15 more minutes over medium heat.
Add the celery and dried basil and cook for 15 more minutes. If the beans still aren't soft, you can cook for up to 30 more minutes.

FOR THE QUINOA

Wash the quinoa well under the tap until the water runs clear. This will help reduce the bitterness. Strain well.
Put the quinoa in a pot, add the vegetable stock, season to taste and bring to a boil. Cover and cook over medium heat for 15 minutes, until the quinoa is translucent. Open the pot, cover with a clean towel, return the lid and let rest for at least 15 minutes.
Serve the quinoa in a deep dish, with the fasulye and cooking juices over it, as a main course or a side dish.

المقادير

(لـ 6 وجبات)

للفاصولياء

2 كوب فاصولياء بيضاء يابسة
1 كيس باكينج باودر
4 ملعقة كبيرة معجون البندورة
6 كوب مرق خضار (الوصفة صفحة 161)
ملح وفلفل أسود حسب الرغبة
3 سيقان كرفس مقطع لمكعبات
1 معلقة كبيرة ريحان مجفف

للكينوا

2 كوب كينوا بيضاء
4 كوب مرق خضار (الوصفة صفحة 161)
ملح وفلفل أسود وأبيض حسب الرغبة

طريقة التحضير

الفاصولياء

تُنقع الفاصولياء البيضاء في الماء ليلة كاملة أو لمدة 8 ساعات على الأقل (من المفضل وضعها في الثلاجة في فصل الصيف)، ثم تُغسَل وتُصفّى. تُوضع الفاصولياء في قدر مع لترين من الماء والباكينج باودر وتُطهى لمدة ساعة. بعدها تُصفى الفاصولياء وتضاف الى القدر مع مرق الخضار ومعجون البندورة، وتُترك على النار حتى تغلي. تُخفَّف الحرارة، وتُغطَّى القدر وتُترك لمدة ساعة تقريبًا حتى تنضج. يُنثر الملح والفلفل الأسود والابيض بعد ربع ساعة من بداية الطهي، ويُضاف الكرفس قبل ربع ساعة من انتهائه. إذا لم تنضج الفاصولياء بعد مضي ساعة، تُطهى لنصف ساعة أخرى.

الكينوا

تُغسل حبوب الكينوا وتُوضع في قدر مع مرق الخضار، ويُضاف إليها الملح والفلفل الأسود. تُخفَّف الحرارة وتُغطَّى القدر وتُترك على نار هادئة لمدة ربع ساعة حتى تصبح شفافة. يُرفع الغطاء عن القدر وتُوضَع عليها فوطة مطبخ نظيفة ثم تُغطَّى وتُترَك جانبًا لمدة ربع ساعة.

تُسكَب الفاصولياء والكينوا في صحن عميق، وتُقدَّم كطبق رئيسي أو ثانوي.

Prague

براغ

|121

# INGREDIENTS

(Serves 4)

**SAUCE**

5 very ripe tomatoes
1 cup ripe cherry tomatoes, halved
2 tablespoon olive oil
1 large onion, diced
3 garlic cloves, sliced
2 tablespoon tomato paste
¼ cup fresh spearmint, chopped
Salt and pepper

**EGG SUBSTITUTE**

**whites**: 1 cup soy beans, cooked and blended
in a food processor (add a ¼ cup
water to process) OR
1 pack soft tofu, mashed
**yolks**: ½ cup lentil flour (or chickpea flour),
mixed with ½ cup water
1 tablespoon kala namek

**SERVING**

¼ cup fresh parsley, chopped
1 tablespoon fresh za'atar

# PREPARATION

**FOR THE SAUCE**

Using a food processor, puree the tomatoes.
In a deep pan, heat the olive oil and fry the onion
until golden. Add the garlic and fry for one more
minute. Add the pureed tomatoes, the cherry
tomatoes and the tomato paste, and season to
taste. Stir well and bring to a boil. Cover the pot,
lower the heat and cook for 10 more minutes.
Add the spearmint to the pot and stir.

**FOR EGG SUBSTITUTE**

**Whites:** Make 4 circular holes in the sauce, about
4 cm (2 inches) in circumference. Pour ¼ of the soy
paste (or tofu) into each.
**Yolks:** Make a small circular hole in each of the
'whites' and pour 1½ spoonfuls of the mixture into
each. Sprinkle ¼ spoonful of kala namek salt over
each 'egg', cover the pan and cook for 10 more
minutes over low heat, until the egg substitutes
thicken and become firm.

**FOR SERVING**

Sprinkle parsley and za'atar on the shakshuka and
serve hot with sliced bread, tahini sauce, green

## المقادير

(لـ 4 وجبات)

**للصلصة**

5 حبات بندورة حمراء كاملة النضج
1 كوب بندورة شيري مقطعة لأنصاف
2 ملعقة كبيرة زيت زيتون
1 بصلة كبيرة مقطّعة لمكعبات
3 فصوص ثوم مفرومة
2 ملعقة كبيرة معجون البندورة
ملح وفلفل أسود حسب الرغبة
¼ كوب نعنع مفروم

**بديل البيض**

**البياض:** 1 كوب فول صويا مطهو ومطحون
بالخلاط مع ربع كوب ماء
أو رزمة توفو طري ومهروس
**الصفار:** ½ كوب طحين العدس
(أو طحين الحمص)
مع ½ كوب ماء
1 ملعقة كبيرة ملح أسود
(كالا ناميك، يعطي نكهة البيض)

**للتقديم**

¼ كوب بقدونس مفروم
1 ملعقة كبيرة زعتر أخضر

## طريقة التحضير

**الصلصة**

تُهرَس حبات البندورة في الخلاط الكهربائي. يُقلى البصل بزيت
الزيتون في مقلاة كبيرة وعميقة حتى يصبح لونه ذهبيًا، يُضاف الثوم
ويُقلّب مع البصل لدقيقة أخرى، ثم تُضاف البندورة المهروسة
وأنصاف الشيري ومعجون البندورة والملح والفلفل. يُحرّك المزيج حتى
يغلي، ثم تُخفَّف الحرارة وتُغطّى المقلاة وتُترك على نار هادئة لمدة عشر
دقائق، ومن بعدها يُضاف النعنع.

**بديل البيض**

**البياض:** نكوّر حفرة في الخليط قطرها 4 سم تقريبا، نضع فيها ¼
كوب من خلطة الصويا أو التوفو.
**الصفار:** نكوّر حفرة صغيرة في بديل البياض ونعبئها بملعقة ونصف
من خليط الصفار.
بهذه الطريقة نكوّن أربع "بيضات"، ثم نرشّ ربع ملعقة من الملح
الأسود (كالا ناميك) على كل "بيضة". نغطي المقلاة ونتركها على نار
هادئة لمدة 10 دقائق حتى يتماسك بديل البيض.

**التقديم**

نرش البقدونس والزعتر على الشكشوكة ونقدّمها ساخنة مع الخبز،
بجانب صلصة الطحينة وسلطة الخضار والزيتون.

# SHAKSHUKA | الشكشوكة

Ask any Israeli what the second most popular dish in Israel is (after hummus, naturally), and they'll quickly answer: shakshuka. But they might be less enthusiastic about vegan shakshuka, since traditionally, shakshuka is made with eggs. Well, here you have a completely vegan shakshuka. In order to get the authentic taste, you have to take a trip to the natural food store and buy kala namek, black Himalayan salt, which gives an egg-like flavor. But you can also make an amazing shakshuka without it. The inspiration for this charming recipe comes from the Facebook group, Vegan Cooking, where I met talented vegan cooks who share their experiences with people converting to a vegan diet. A special thanks to Mor Elbaz and Tal Mizrahi, who had the original idea for this recipe.

**Tahini Sauce:** Combine ½ cup tahini, ¼ cup cold water, juice from ½ lemon and a teaspoon of salt, and mix until uniform. You can add water or tahini, depending on how thick you want the sauce, or spices and herbs for variety and color.

if you don't keep products such as lentil flour, kala namek or soy beans at home, you can also blend 1 pack of soft tofu with salt, pepper and a bit of turmeric, and use the mixture as an egg substitute.

TIP!

لدى تحضير بديل البيض يمكن استبدال طحين العدس وملح كالا ناميك وفول الصويا إذا لم تتوفر. بالتوفو الطري المطحون. الملح والفلفل الأسود والقليل من الكركم لإضفاء اللون الأصفر.

# SHORBET AL-'ADS WO MUHAMMARA
## RED LENTIL SOUP AND RED PEPPER PASTRIES

شوربة العدس والمحمّرة

The Arab cuisine has a variety of inherently vegan dishes that not only require no substitutes or new habits, but almost beg you to try them. Here is a wonderful example of two dishes that, together, create a particularly well-balanced and colorful meal, equal parts healthy and unapologetically hedonistic. The shorbet al-'ads, a red lentil soup, offers the nutrition and the muhammara pastries, which almost look like tiny pizzas, offer the fun. Ahmar is 'red' in Arabic, and these pastries get their name from their reddish color – they're covered with a hot, red pepper paste. Just smelling them, before they're even out of the oven, is guaranteed to whet your appetite.

# INGREDIENTS

(Serves 4-6)

## SOUP

2 cups red lentils
7 cups vegetables stock (see recipe on page 161)
1 medium onion, diced
1 medium carrot, diced
Juice from ½ large lemon

## MUHAMMARA

3 cups flour
1 teaspoon dry yeast
1 tablespoon sugar (white or brown)
1 cup water
1 teaspoon salt

## PEPPER PASTE

4 red bell peppers
1 garlic clove
1 onion
½ cup ground walnuts
1 tablespoon olive oil
1 teaspoon cumin
¼ cup pine nuts, roasted
Salt

# PREPARATION

## FOR THE SOUP

Wash the lentils well and put them in a large pot. Add the vegetable stock, the carrot and the onion and bring to a boil. Season with salt, cover the pot, lower the heat and cook for 40 minutes. Add the lemon juice and blend the soup until smooth. Adjust seasoning to taste.

## FOR THE MUHAMMARA DOUGH

In a large bowl combine all of the dry ingredients. Add the water gradually, kneading well for 10 minutes, until uniform. Cover in shrink wrap. Put a towel over the bowl and let the dough rise until it doubles in volume – about 3 hours in winter and an hour to 90 minutes in summer.

## FOR THE PEPPER PASTE

In a food processor, combine the peppers, onion and garlic and process until smooth. Move to a strainer and press to remove as much of the liquid as possible. Move to a bowl and mix well with the walnuts, olive oil, cumin and salt.

## TO ASSEMBLE THE MUHAMMARA

Divide the dough into 16 equal balls. Using a rolling pin, roll out each ball into circles 2 cm (1 inch) thick and 7 cm (3 inches) in circumference. Spread the pepper paste on the circles so they're evenly covered. Arrange the circles on baking sheets lined with parchment paper. Keep about 2 cm (1 inch) of space between them – they'll expand during baking. Bake for 5-7 minutes, until the dough browns. I recommend that you bake in batches, one sheet at a time.

Garnish the muhammara pastries with roasted pine nuts and serve with the soup (it's best to prepare the soup in advance and heat it just before serving).

## الشوربة

يُغسَل العدس جيّدًا ويوضع في قدر عميقة، ويُضاف إليه مرق الخضار ومكعّبات البصل ويُترَك ليغلي. يُنثَر الملح وتُغطَّى القدر وتترك على نار هادئة لمدة 40 دقيقة. يُضاف للشوربة عصير الليمون ثم تُطحن بالخلاط الكهربائي للحصول على قوام متجانس وأملس. يمكن إضافة الملح حسب الحاجة.

## عجينة المحمّرة

تُخلَط جميع المكوّنات الجافة في وعاء، ويُضاف الماء تدريجيًا أثناء العجن. نستمر بالعجن لمدة عشر دقائق حتى الحصول على عجينة طرية ومتجانسة. تُغلَّف العجينة بالنايلون وتُغطَّى بفوطة وتُترَك حتى يتضاعف حجمها (ثلاث ساعات في الشتاء وساعة ونصف في الصيف).

## معجون الفلفل

تُطحَن حبات الفلفل منزوعة البذور مع البصل والثوم في الخلاط الكهربائي، وتُصفَّى من السوائل، ثمّ يُضاف إليها الجوز، الملح، الزيت والكمون، وتُخلَط المكوّنات جيّدًا.

## المحمّرة

يُقطَّع العجين إلى 16 كرة متساوية، وتُفرَد كلٌّ منها إلى دائرة صغيرة سمكها 2 سم وقطرها 7 سم. تُدهَن كل دائرة بمعجون الفلفل، وتُرتَّب الأرغفة الصغيرة في صينية مغطاة بورق الخبز مع الحفاظ على بعد 2 سم فيما بينها حتى لا تلتصق. تُخبَز في فرن مسخَّن مسبقًا على حرارة 180 درجة لمدة 5-7 دقائق حتى تصبح ذهبية اللون.

تُزيَّن المحمرة بالصنوبر المحمَّص وتُقدَّم بجانب شوربة العدس (يُفضَّل تحضير الشوربة مسبقا، وتسخينها عند التقديم).

## للشوربة

2 كوب عدس أحمر مجروش
7 كوب مرق خضار (الوصفة صفحة 161)
1 بصلة متوسطة مقطعة لمكعبات
1 جزرة متوسطة مقطعة لمكعبات
ملح حسب الرغبة
عصير نصف ليمونة كبيرة

## للمحمّرة (١٦ قطعة)

3 كوب طحين
1 ملعقة صغيرة خميرة
1 ملعقة كبيرة سكر أبيض أو بني
1 ملعقة صغيرة ملح
1 كوب ماء

## معجون الفلفل

4 حبات فلفل أحمر
1 فص ثوم
1 بصلة
½ كوب جوز نيء مطحون
1 ملعقة كبيرة زيت زيتون
1 ملعقة صغيرة كمون
ملح حسب الرغبة
¼ كوب صنوبر محمّص

# INGREDIENTS

(Serves 4-6)

### SOY CHUNKS

30 large soy chunks
   (available in natural food stores)*
4 cups vegetable stock (see recipe on page 161)
2 tablespoon olive oil
1 cup barbecue sauce
3 tablespoon soy sauce
2 tablespoon hot paprika

### STEW

3 cups vegetable stock
3 tablespoon tomato paste
1½ cups green peas, fresh or frozen
3 carrots, diced to medium size
Salt and pepper

# PREPARATION

### FOR THE SOY CHUNKS

In a deep pot, cook the soy chunks in the vegetable stock for about 30 minutes, until soft. Move them to a strainer and squeeze out the excess fluids.
In a wide pan, heat the olive oil and lightly saute the soy chunks. Add the sauces and paprika, stir well and cook over medium heat for 10 minutes, until all the liquids have been absorbed. Let cool.

### FOR THE STEW

In another pot, bring all of the ingredients to a boil. Cover with the lid and cook for 30 minutes over medium heat, until the vegetable soften. Taste, adjust seasoning and add the cooked soy chunks. Serve with white rice.

*You can substitute with 300 g (about 10.5 oz) seitan, homemade (see recipe on page 158) or store-bought, diced into 30 medium sized cubes.

---

# المقادير

(لـ 4-6 وجبات)

### لقطع الصويا

30 قطع صويا كبيرة الحجم
(تجدونها في محلات المنتجات الطبيعية)*
4 كوب مرق خضار
(الوصفة صفحة 161)
2 ملعقة كبيرة زيت زيتون
1 كوب صلصة باربكيو
3 ملعقة كبيرة صلصة الصويا
1 ملعقة كبيرة ببريكا حارة

### البازيلاء الصويا

3 كوب مرق خضار
3 ملعقة كبيرة معجون البندورة
1½ كوب بازيلاء (طازجة أو مثلَّجة)
3 حبات جزر مقطعة لمكعبات
ملح وفلفل أسود حسب الرغبة

# طريقة التحضير

### قطع الصويا

تُسلَق قطع الصويا مع مرق الخضار لمدة نصف ساعة حتى تنضج، ثم تُصفّى من السوائل.
في مقلاة كبيرة ساخنة تُقلى قطع الصويا بزيت الزيتون وتُضاف إليها صلصة الباربكيو والببريكا، وتُترَك على نار متوسطة لمدة ربع ساعة حتى تجفّ السوائل، وتُترَك جانبًا لتبرد.

### البازيلاء

توضَع البازيلاء في قدر المرق ويُضاف إليها معجون البندورة وقطع الجزر، وتُترَك لتغلي لمدة نصف ساعة على نار متوسطة. تُنثَر البهارات في نهاية الطهي وتُرفَع عن النار. تُضاف قطع الصويا للقدر وتُحرَّك مع بقية المحتويات.
تُقدَّم مع الأرز الأبيض.

*من الممكن استبدالها بـ 300 غرام بروتين القمح سواء من صنع بيتي (الوصفة صفحة 158) أو جاهز بالنكهة الطبيعية، وتقطيعه إلى 30 مكعبًا صغيرًا.

# BAZEILA MA' SOYA 'GOULASH' WITH PEAS AND SOY CHUNKS

البازيلاء مع قطع الصويا

Goulash, the Hungarian national dish, has also found its way into the Arab cuisine, where it received a new twist: peas and carrots replace meat and potatoes in the red paprika sauce. Not exactly the classic recipe, but rich in its own way. The vegan cuisine, which reinvents itself every day anew, utilizes a lot of meat substitutes in traditional dishes. It isn't easy to let go of the familiar, traditional flavors, so we learn to be inventive! Try preparing goulash with large soy chunks, and you'll find out they're perfect for the job – they easily take on deep flavors such as barbecue sauce, and slow cooking them in vegetable stock will make them juicy.

Prague براغ

# KUFTA BI TEHINA
## SEITAN MEATBALLS IN TAHINI

الكفتة بالطحينة

When I was just starting out as a vegan, I found myself missing the traditional, meat-based dishes of the Arab cuisine. I consulted a lot of vegans, and looked for creative ideas of my own to reproduce them in a loving, compassionate and healthy way. The kufta is a traditional meat dish with a texture reminiscent of the kebab, but prepared and seasoned differently. The two main types are sinyiet al-kufta (see recipe on page 136) and kufta bi tehina, here is a seitan-based vegan version.

# INGREDIENTS

(Makes 8 units)

1 cup vegan mince, homemade
  (see recipe on page 160) or store-bought
1 medium potato, boiled and cooled
1 large onion, chopped
¼ cup spring onion, chopped
¼ cup parsley or coriander
¼ breadcrumbs
2 tablespoon olive oil
¼ teaspoon sweet paprika
¼ teaspoon hot paprika
¼ teaspoon dry garlic powder
Salt and pepper
Deep-frying oil

TAHINI

1 cup tahini
2 cups water
1 large lemon
Salt

SERVING

¼ cup chopped parsley
1 tablespoon roasted pine nuts
1 tablespoon nigella seeds (optional)

# PREPARATION

FOR THE SEITAN MEATBALLS

In a food processor, blend the vegan mince, the potato, the onion and the spring onion. Move to a bowl and add the rest of the ingredients, except for the oil. Mix until uniform. If the mixture is too soft you can add more breadcrumbs.
Make balls about 7 cm (3 inches) in diameter and 2 cm (1 inch) thick. Heat some oil in a non-stick pan and fry the balls for 5-7 minutes on each side, until brown. Keep the pan covered while frying.

FOR THE TAHINI SAUCE

In a bowl, mix all of the ingredients until you have a uniform sauce. The texture should be thinner than usual.
Heat the sauce in a wide, deep pot over low heat, stirring lightly, for 10 minutes. Be careful not to overcook, or the tahini might separate. Add the kufta, sprinkle parsley, pine nuts and nigella, and serve immediately.

## طريقة التحضير

يُطحن بروتين الصويا والبصل بنوعيه في خلاط كهربائي، ويُنقَل الخليط إلى وعاء. تُضاف كل مكوّنات الكفتة للخليط، ما عدا زيت القلي، وتُقلَّب حتى الحصول على قوام متجانس.

تُحضَّر من الخليط كرات قطرها 7 سم وسمكها 2 سم، وتُقلى في القليل من الزيت في مقلاة غير لاصقة ومغطّاة، لمدة 5-7 دقائق من كل جهة حتى تنضج.

تُخلَط كل مكوّنات الصلصة في وعاء حتى الحصول على قوام متجانس ورخو بعض الشيء. تُغلى صلصة الطحينة في قدر، وتُحرَّك عدة مرات لمدة عشر دقائق، مع مراعاة عدم تفتّتها أثناء التسخين. تُضاف الكفتة إلى الصلصة، ويُنثَر عليها البقدونس والصنوبر والقزحة.

## المقادير

(ل 8 أقراص)

1 كوب بروتين الصويا المطحون سواء من صنع بيتي (الوصفة صفحة 160) أو جاهز بالنكهة الطبيعية
1 حبة بطاطا متوسطة مسلوقة
1 بصلة كبيرة مفرومة
¼ كوب بصل أخضر مفروم
¼ كوب بقدونس/كزبرة مفروم/ة
¼ كوب فتات الخبز
2 ملعقة كبيرة زيت زيتون
¼ ملعقة صغيرة ببريكا حلوة
¼ ملعقة صغيرة ببريكا حارة
¼ ملعقة بودرة الثوم
ملح وفلفل أسود حسب الرغبة
زيت للقلي

1 كوب طحينة
2 كوب ماء
ملح
عصير من 1 ليمونة كبيرة

¼ كوب بقدونس مفروم
1 ملعقة كبيرة صنوبر محمّص
1 ملعقة صغيرة قزحة (اختياري)

# INGREDIENTS

(Serves 4-6 [a 20X20 cm (8X8 inches) baking

500 g (17 oz) red lentils, soaked overnight
1 cup vegan mince, homemade
  (see recipe on page 160) or store-bought
1 large onion
1 tablespoon soy sauce
1 tablespoon barbecue sauce
½ cup parsley, chopped
¼ teaspoon sweet paprika
¼ teaspoon hot paprika
Salt and pepper

TOPPING

1 tomato, sliced
1 onion, sliced

SAUCE

½ cup vegetable stock (see recipe on page 161)
1 tablespoon tomato paste

# PREPARATION

Preheat the oven to 180 degrees C (350 degrees F).
Blend the lentils, vegan mince, onion, soy sauce and
barbecue sauce in a food processor, to a uniform
paste. Add the parsley and spices and mix well with
your hands or a large spoon.
Transfer the mixture to an oiled dish.
Arrange the tomato and onion slices over the
mixture, bake for 20-30 minutes, until brown and
solid.

FOR THE SAUCE

Mix the vegetable stock with the tomato paste in a
small pot over low heat, and bring to a boil.
Pour the sauce over the siniya and serve hot, with
tahini sauce and fresh, chopped salad.

المقادير

(لـ 4-6 وجبات، لصينية 20×20 سم)

500 غرام عدس أحمر مجروش منقوع
ليلة كاملة
1 كوب بروتين الصويا المطحون سواء من
صنع بيتي (الوصفة صفحة 160) أو جاهز
بالنكهة الطبيعية
1 بصلة كبيرة
1 ملعقة كبيرة صلصة صويا
1 ملعقة كبيرة صلصة باربكيو
½ كوب بقدونس مفروم
¼ملعقة صغيرة ببريكا حلوة
¼ملعقة صغيرة ببريكا حارة
ملح وفلفل أسود حسب الرغبة

للطبقة العليا

1 بندورة مقطّعة إلى شرائح
1 بصلة مقطّعة إلى شرائح

للصلصة

½ كوب مرق الخضار
1 ملعقة معجون البندورة

طريقة التحضير

يُطحَن العدس المجروش في الخلاط الكهربائي مع بروتين الصويا،
البصل، صلصة الصويا والباربكيو حتى الحصول على قوام متجانس،
ثم يُضاف البقدونس والبهارات وتُخلَط المكوّنات جيّدًا.
تُوضَع الكفتة في صينية فرن مدهونة بالقليل من الزيت، وتُوضع
فوقها شرائح البصل والبندورة وتُدخَل إلى فرن مسخَّن مسبقًا على
حرارة 180درجة لمدة 20-30 دقيقة، حتى يصبح لون الكفتة داكنًا
ويتقلّص حجمها.

الصلصة

يُطهى المرق ومعجون البندورة في قدر على نار هادئة حتى يغلي.
تُسكَب الصلصة فوق صينية الكفتة وتُقدَّم ساخنة مع صلصة
الطحينة والسلطة الطازجة.

# SINYET AL-KUFTA | صينية الكفتة

The original siniya is a pastry with minced meat, tahini and vegetables. in this version I replaced the meat with vegan mince and red lentils, which add texture and nutritional value, and left the pastry light, without the baked tahini. You can, of course, serve it with a side of tahini sauce.

# 'ADS WO MAKARONA LENTILS AND MACARONI

العدس مع المعكرونة

In Arabic, lentils are sometimes called "the poor man's meat." They are cheap and readily available, and you can cook them into a variety of nutritious, filling meatless meals – from lentil soup to majadara.
Try this thick, lemony sauce over broad pasta, and you have an original, charming rural dish.

# INGREDIENTS

(Serves 4-6)

1 pack pasta (500 g, about 1 lb),
   preferably linguini or spaghetti

## LENTIL SAUCE

1 cup black lentils
3 cups vegetable stock
   (see recipe on page 161)
1 small onion, chopped
1 teaspoon cumin
Salt and pepper
Juice from ½ large lemon
Lemon slices

# PREPARATION

## FOR THE LEMON SAUCE

Put the lentils in a pot, add the vegetable stock
and onion and bring to a boil. Cook over a
medium heat for 30-40 minutes, until the lentils
soften. Add the lemon juice and adjust seasoning
to taste.
While the sauce is cooking, boil the pasta
according to the instructions.
Keep ¼ cup of the sauce separate (so when
you serve, some of the lentils will be whole) and
blend the rest to a uniform paste.

## FOR SERVING

Pour the smooth paste over the hot pasta, add
the lentils you kept, and garnish with lemon
slices. You can also grate some fresh carrot on
top.

# المقادير

(لـ 4-6 وجبات)

1 رزمة معكرونة (500 غرام)

## صلصة العدس الحامض

1 كوب عدس أسود صحيح
3 كوب مرق خضار
(الوصفة صفحة 161)
1 بصلة صغيرة
1 ملعقة صغيرة كمون
ملح وفلفل أسود حسب الرغبة
عصير نصف ليمونة كبيرة
شرائح ليمون للتقديم

# طريقة التحضير

## صلصة العدس الحامض

يُوضَع العدس في قدر ويُضاف إليه مرق الخضار والبصل والبهارات
ويُترَك حتى يغلي. تُخفَّف النار، وتُترَك القدر على نار متوسطة لمدة
30-40 دقيقة حتى ينضج العدس، ثم يُضاف عصير الليمون. يمكن
تعديل المذاق بإضافة التوابل حسب الحاجة.
تُسلَق المعكرونة حسب الإرشادات الواردة على الغلاف. من المفضَّل
البدء بالسلق قبل وقت قصير من نضج الصلصة.
نحتفظ بربع كوب من الصلصة جانبًا (ليكون لدينا القليل من
العدس غير المطحون)، ثم تُطحن المقادير في الخلاط الكهربائي حتى
الحصول على هريس.

## التقديم

تُسكَب الصلصة على المعكرونة الساخنة، ويُضاف إليها القليل من
العدس الصحيح الذي وضعناه جانبًا وبعض شرائح الليمون، كما
يمكن إضافة الجزر المبروش.

# SHUSHBARAK DUMPLINGS IN YOGHURT SAUCE | الشوشبرك

This is one of the Arab cuisine's grandest dishes. It is the pride of many cooks, since it requires a certain skill, and a lot of effort. The traditional recipe has the dumplings filled with meat and swimming in a warm, sour yoghurt sauce – perhaps the farthest you can get from vegan. But I missed the flavors from home so much that I had to try and make a vegan version. I replaced the meat filling with fried zucchini and onion, made a vegan yoghurt sauce, and even added a new twist to the dough: beet juice. It gives the dumplings their attractive pinkish tone.

# INGREDIENTS

(Serves 4-6)

DOUGH

2 cups flour
½ cup water
⅓ cup oil
Juice from ¼ beet
¼ teaspoon salt

FILLING

1 small onion
1 zucchini
1 tablespoon olive oil
Salt and pepper

YOGHURT SAUCE

5 cups vegan yoghurt, homemade
    (see recipe on page 162) or store-bought
1 tablespoon cornstarch
½ cup cold water
Juice from 3 large lemons
Salt

# PREPARATION

FOR THE DOUGH

Preheat the oven to 180 degrees C (350 degrees F). In a bowl, combine all of the ingredients and knead to a uniform, pinkish dough. Wrap with shrink wrap and refrigerate for 30 minutes.

FOR THE FILLING

Dice the zucchini and onion to small cubes. In a pan, heat the olive oil and fry the onion over medium heat for 5 minutes, until golden. Add the zucchini, salt and pepper to taste and fry for 10 more minutes, stirring constantly.

THE ASSEMBLE

Divide the dough into 2 equal parts, and roll each to about 2 cm (1 inch) thick. Using a round cutter (or a cup), make 3-4 cm (1½ inch) circles.
In the center of each circle put a teaspoonful of the filling, fold in half, and pinch the ends shut. Put the dumplings on a baking sheet lined with parchment paper and bake for 15 minutes.

FOR THE YOGHURT SAUCE

Pour the yoghurt into a deep pot, and add a cup of boiling water. In another cup dissolve the cornstarch in ½ cup cold water and pour it in the pot. Add the lemon juice and salt to taste and bring to a boil. Carefully add the dumplings and cook over low heat for about 20 minutes. Serve hot, garnished with roasted pine nuts and chopped parsley.

## طريقة التحضير

### المقادير

(لـ 4-6 وجبات)

### العجينة

**للعجينة**

تُخلَط جميع مكوّنات العجينة في وعاء حتى الحصول على عجينة طرية ورديّة اللون، ثم تُغلَّف بالنايلون وتُوضَع في الثلاجة لمدة نصف ساعة لترتاح.

- 2 كوب طحين
- ½ كوب ماء
- ⅓ كوب زيت نباتي
- عصير ربع حبة شمندر
- ¼ ملعقة صغيرة ملح

### للحشوة

**للحشوة**

يُقلى البصل بزيت الزيتون لمدة 5 دقائق حتى يذبل ويصبح ذهبيّ اللون. تُضاف مكعبات الكوسا للبصل ويُنثَر الملح والفلفل الأسود، وتُترَك على النار لمدة 10 دقائق مع الاستمرار بالتحريك.

- 1 بصلة صغيرة مقطعة لمكعبات
- 1 كوسا أو زوكيني مقطعة لمكعبات
- 1 ملعقة كبيرة زيت زيتون
- ملح وفلفل أسود حسب الرغبة

### تحضير الشوشبرك

**لصلصة اللبن**

تُقطَّع العجينة إلى نصفين، ويُفرد كل قسم بواسطة الشوبك حتى يكون سمكه 2 سم. تُقطَّع العجينة إلى دوائر قطرها 3-4 سم بواسطة أداة خاصة أو كأس.

توضَع ملعقة صغيرة من الحشوة في وسط كل دائرة، وتُطوى أطرافها على شكل نصف دائرة، ويُضغَط عليها لإغلاقها. تُخبز المعجنات في فرن مسخّن على حرارة 180 درجة لمدة ربع ساعة حتى تصبح ذهبيّة اللون.

- 5 كوب لبن نباتي جاهز (الوصفة صفحة 162)
- 1 ملعقة كبيرة نشاء
- ½ كوب ماء بارد
- عصير 3 حبات ليمون كبير الحجم
- ملح حسب الرغبة

### صلصة اللبن

يُسكَب اللبن النباتي في قدر ويُضاف إليه كوب من الماء المغلي. يُذوَّب النشاء في نصف كوب من الماء البارد على حدة، ثم يُضاف إلى قدر اللبن. يُسكَب عصير الليمون والملح ويُترَك المزيج حتى يغلي. تُضاف معجّنات الشوشبرك إلى اللبن وتُطهى على نار خفيفة لمدة 20 دقيقة. يسكَب الشوشبرك في طبق ويُنثَر عليه الصنوبر المحمّص وحفنة من البقدونس المفروم ويُقدَّم ساخنًا.

# 'IJET AL-BROCCOLI | عجة البروكلي

Juicy broccoli fritters you can easily make without any eggs. How? Replace the eggs with a quick, soft tofu-based mixture, an excellent solution I learned from Smadar Bar Yochai during my wanderings through the internet's vegan cooking pages. You can use it to prepare fritters of other vegetables, too, but beware: it's addictive and fried!

# INGREDIENTS

(Serves 4-6)

BROCCOLI FRITTERS

1 medium head of broccoli,
   broken into florets
¾ cup lentil flour or chickpea flour
½ large onion, finely chopped
1 garlic clove, crushed
¼ cup parsley, chopped
¼ cup spearmint, chopped
2 tablespoon olive oil
½ teaspoon baking soda
¼ cup water
1 teaspoon cumin
1 teaspoon sweet paprika
Salt and pepper

EGG SUBSTITUTE

80 g (3 oz) soft tofu
2 tablespoon flour
2 tablespoon water
1½ tablespoon oil
½ teaspoon baking powder
Deep-frying oil

# PREPARATION

Cook the broccoli in plenty of water over low heat
for 20 minutes, until soft. Strain the water and puree
the broccoli to a smooth paste. Cool well. Mix the
broccoli paste with the rest of the fritter ingredients
in a large bowl.
In a food processor, blend all of the ingredients for
the egg substitute into a smooth paste. Add it to the
broccoli paste and stir until uniform. If it's too runny,
you can add some flour and if it's too dry – a little
cold water.
Make round fritters, 6 cm (2½ in) in diameter and 2
cm (1 in) thick.
In a pan, heat the frying oil and fry the fritters until
golden, about 3-4 minutes on each side.
Serve hot with tahini sauce or vegan yoghurt and a
lot of salad.

Tahini Sauce: Combine ½ cup tahini, ¼ cup cold water, juice from ½ lemon and a teaspoon of
salt, and mix until uniform. You can add water or tahini, depending on how thick you want the
sauce, or spices and herbs for variety and color.

# المقادير

(لـ 4-6 وجبات)

لأقراص البروكلي

1 بروكلي متوسط مقطّع إلى زهرات
¾ كوب طحين عدس او حمص
½ بصلة مفرومة فرمًا ناعمًا
1 فص ثوم مهروس
¼ كوب بقدونس مفروم
¼ كوب نعنع مفروم
2 ملعقة زيت زيتون
½ ملعقة صغيرة بيكربونات الصودا
¼ كوب ماء
1 ملعقة صغيرة كمون
1 ملعقة صغيرة ببريكا حلوة
ملح وفلفل أسود حسب الرغبة

بديل البيض

80 غرام توفو طري
2 ملعقة كبيرة طحين
2 ملعقة كبيرة ماء
1½ ملعقة كبيرة زيت نباتي
½ ملعقة صغيرة باكينج باودر
زيت لقلي نصف عميق

# طريقة التحضير

تُغمَر زهرات البروكلي بالماء وتُسلَق في قدر عميقة لمدة 20 دقيقة على
نار متوسطة حتى تطرى. يُصفّى البروكلي من الماء ويُهرَس في الخلاط
الكهربائي، ويُترَك ليبرد ثمّ يُخلَط مع بقية مكوّنات أقراص البروكلي.
تُطحَن مواد "بديل البيض" حتى الحصول على هريس، وتُضاف إلى
خليط أقراص البروكلي وتُحرّك جيدًا. إذا كان القوام رخوًا يُضاف
إليه القليل من الطحين وإذا كان جامدًا يُضاف إليه القليل من الماء
البارد.

تُحضَّر من الخليط قلوب قطرها 6 سم وسمكها 2 سم، وتُقلى في زيت
ساخن يصل إلى نصف عمق المقلاة، لمدة 3-4 دقائق تقريبًا من كل
جانب، حتى تصبح ذهبيّة اللون.

تُقدَّم ساخنة مع صلصة الطحينة أو اللبن النباتي وسلطة الخضار.

# INGREDIENTS

(Makes a 20X20 cm [8X8 in] dish)

## DOUGH

2 cups flour
½ cup sugar
½ cup thin oatmeal
¾ cup refined coconut oil, liquid
Zest from ½ lemon

## FILLING

1 cup jam (your preferred kind)
1 tablespoon cinnamon
2 tablespoon crushed walnuts
¼ cup raisins (optional)

# PREPARATION

Preheat the oven to 180 degrees C (350 degrees F).
In a bowl, combine all of the ingredients except the
lemon zest, and knead for at least 5 minutes, until
uniform. Add the lemon zest and divide the dough
into two equal halves.
Put one in an oiled dish. Spread the dough with your
hands to cover the dish uniformly.
In another bowl, combine the ingredients for the
filling.  Spread the filling evenly over the dough.
Grate the second half of the dough over the filling,
so the jam is completely covered with dough
crumbs.
Bake for 20-30 minutes, until the mabrusha turns
golden, or until you can insert a tooth pick and it
comes out dry. Cut into squares while still warm.

المقادير

(لصينية 20×20 سم)

للعجين

2 كوب طحين
½ كوب سكر
½ كوب شوفان
¾ زيت جوز الهند سائل
برش قشرة نصف ليمونة

الحشوة

1 كوب مربى
1ملعقة كبيرة قرفة
2 ملعقة كبيرة جوز نيء مطحون
¼ كوب زبيب (اختياري)

طريقة التحضير

تُخلَط في وعاء جميع مكوّنات العجين، عدا برش الليمون، وتُعجَن
لمدة 5 دقائق حتى الحصول على قوام متجانس. يُضاف برش الليمون
وتُقطَّع العجينة لنصفين.
يُوضَع نصف العجينة في صينية فرن مدهونة بالقليل من الزيت،
وبواسطة الضغط بالأصابع واليدين تُوزَّع على الصينية بشكل
متساوٍ. تُخلَط جميع مكوّنات الحشوة وتُوزَّع فوق العجينة
بالتساوي. يُبرَش النصف الثاني من العجينة ويُنثَر فوق الحشوة حتى
يغطيها تمامًا. تُخبَز المبروشة في فرن مسخَّن مسبقًا على حرارة 180
درجة لمدة
20-30 دقيقة حتى تصبح ذهبيّة اللون. يمكن التأكد من نضج
المبروشة من خلال غرزها بعود خشبي، فإذا خرج جافًا تكون الكعكة
قد نضجت. تُقطَّع المبروشة إلى مربعات وهي ساخنة.

# MABRUSHA JAM COOKIES | المبروشة

This isn't an original Arab recipe. You can find versions of it in almost every cuisine. But the Arab cuisine did give it the splendid name "mabrusha," derived from the same root as the verb for "to grate," because the top layer is made of grated dough. I remember my mother eagerly awaiting the short apricot season, so she could prepare them with fresh jam, but you can use jam of any kind, and get wonderful cookies. I have replaced the classic butter-based dough with a coconut oil-based one, which is healthier and tastier.

# KAA'K AL-EID
## MA'AMOUL
### كعك العيد

Kaa'k al-eid, "holiday cookies," are made of dough and filled with strongly spiced dates. They are also known as khak bajwa or ma'amoul, and are usually served on Muslim holidays.

# INGREDIENTS

(units 30)

½ kg (1 lb) semolina
¼ cup brown sugar
½ cup flour
½ tablespoon baking powder
½ tablespoon vanilla sugar
½ teaspoon ground makhlab (optional, can be found in specialty spice shops)
½ cup non-dairy milk
200 g (7 oz) refined coconut oil

FILLING

250g (9 oz) medjool dates, pitted
50g (2 oz) refined coconut oil
1½ teaspoon ground anise
   (can be found in spice shops)
1½ teaspoon ground nutmeg
½ teaspoon ground cardamom

GARNISH

Caster sugar

# PREPARATION

FOR THE DOUGH

Preheat the oven to 180 degrees C (350 degrees F). In a large bowl, combine all of the dry ingredients. Add the milk and coconut oil and knead until uniform (about 20 minutes). Cover with shrink wrap and let it rest in the refrigerator for at least an hour.

FOR THE FILLING

In a bowl, mix all of the ingredients and knead until uniform and easy to work.

TO ASSEMBLE

Divide the dough into 30 small balls. For each cookie, press the ball into a rectangle. Using your pinky, make a dent in the rectangle and fill it with the date mixture. Close gently with your fingers and make sure the dough is shut tight. Arrange the cookies on a baking sheet lined with parchment paper and bake for 10-12 minutes, until golden but not burnt.
Let cool and, using a small sieve, garnish with caster sugar.

## طريقة التحضير

### طريقة التحضير

تُخلَط جميع مكوّنات العجين الجافة، ثمّ يُضاف إليها زيت جوز الهند السائل والحليب، وتُعجن حتى الحصول على عجينة طرية ومتماسكة (على الأقل 20 دقيقة). تُغطّى العجينة بكيس نايلون أو فوطة مطبخ رطبة، وتُوضع في الثلاجة لمدة ساعة على الأقل حتى ترتاح.

### الحشوة

يُخلَط التمر، زيت جوز الهند، اليانسون، جوزة الطيب والهيل، حتى تتماسك المكوّنات. تُقطَّع العجينة إلى كرات متساوية وتُحشى بالتمر. يمكن ضغط الكرات في قوالب خاصة للحصول على أشكال متنوعة، أو نقشها بالملقط الخاص حسب الرغبة.

يُخبَز الكعك في فرن مسخَّن مسبقا لحرارة 180 درجة، لمدة 12-10 دقيقة حتى يصبح ذهبي اللون (مع مراعاة عدم الخبز المفرط).

للتقديم: يُنثَر السكر الناعم على الكعك بعد أن يبرد.

## المقادير

(لـ 30 كعكة)

### للعجين

500 غرام سميد
¼ كوب سكر بني
½ كوب طحين
½ كيس باكينج باودر
½ كيس سكر فانيليا
½ ملعقة صغيرة محلب (اختياري)
½ كوب (125 مل) حليب الصويا/ اللوز/ الشوفان
200 غرام زيت جوز الهند

### الحشوة

250 غرام تمر منزوع البذور
50 غرام زيت جوز الهند
1½ ملعقة صغيرة يانسون مطحون
1½ ملعقة صغيرة بهار جوزة الطيب
½ ملعقة صغيرة هيل مطحون

### للتزيين

سكر ناعم

**For variety:** You can use ma'amoul tweezers to decorate the cookies with patterns and designs or add walnuts to the filling.

للتنويع: يمكن إضافة الجوز النيئ إلى الحشوة وتشكيل الكعك بأشكال مختلفة، حسب الرغبة.

براغ Prague

# KUBET AL-BATATA
## POTATO KUBEH
كبة البطاطا

This is an easy, vegan, particularly delicious version of the kubeh. When you prepare these dumplings correctly, they have a crunchy crust and juicy filling that melts in your mouth. Even kubbeh traditionalists will fall silent. They'll just be too busy chewing…

# INGREDIENTS

(Makes 10-15 units)

## POTATO DOUGH

3 large potatoes
1 cup bulgur
1 tablespoon olive oil
1 teaspoon red paprika
½ teaspoon turmeric
Salt and pepper

## MUSHROOM STUFFING DOUGH

1 medium onion, finely chopped
1 tablespoon olive oil
250 g (9 oz) champignon mushrooms,
    finely chopped
¼ cup roasted pine nuts
1 teaspoon cinnamon
1 teaspoon cumin
1 teaspoon dry garlic powder
Salt and pepper

## COATING

½ cup tempura mix
Breadcrumbs
Deep-frying oil

# PREPARATION

## FOR THE POTATO DOUGH

Boil the potatoes (without peeling) in a large pot full of water. Cool well, remove the peels and puree until smooth. Mix in the spices and olive oil.
Separately, soak the bulgur in boiling water for 15 minutes. In a food processor, blend the bulgur for about 3 minutes. Add it to the potato mixture and stir well. Refrigerate for 3 hours, to allow the dough to solidify and absorb the flavors.

## FOR THE MUSHROOM STUFFING

In a pan, heat the olive oil and fry the onion until golden. Add the mushrooms, stir and cover for 5 minutes. Add the spices, stir well and cover. Simmer for 5 more minutes over medium heat and add the roasted pine nuts. Cool well.

## TO ASSEMBLE

Make small balls from the mashed potatoes and, using your index finger, create a small dimple in the center of each ball, leaving walls 1-2 cm (½-1 in) thick. Fill each dimple with a spoonful of the mushroom mixture and close well, making sure there aren't any holes. Shape the balls into an ellipsoid with tapering ends.

## FOR THE COATING

Dissolve the tempura mix in ½ cup cold water, and pour into a plate. Pour the breadcrumbs onto a second plate. One by one, dip each kubbeh first in the tempura and then in the breadcrumbs, making sure they're well coated in both. Refrigerate for 30 minutes.
In a large pot, heat the oil and fry the kubbehs for 3-4 minutes, until the crust turns golden. Serve hot with a fresh green salad.

## طريقة التحضير

### لإعداد العجينة

تُسلَق البطاطا بقشرتها في قدر من الماء مع ملعقة ملح، ثم تُقشَّر وتُهرَس. تُخلَط البهارات وتُضاف مع الزيت إلى البطاطا المهروسة. يُخلَط البرغل مع كوب من الماء المغلي ويُترك لمدة ربع ساعة ثم يُطحَن بالخلاط الكهربائي لمدة 3 دقائق. يُخلَط البرغل مع بقية المكوّنات، ويُترك في الثلاجة لمدة ثلاث ساعات لامتصاص النكهات.

### للحشوة

يُقلَى البصل بالزيت حتى يذبل ويصبح ذهبيّ اللون ثمّ يُضاف الفطر وتُغطَّى المقلاة. يُترك الخليط على نار متوسّطة لمدة خمس دقائق، ثم يُحرَّك وتُنثَر عليه بهارات الحشوة والصنوبر المحمّص، ويُترك على نار متوسطة لخمس دقائق أخرى. ومن بعدها يُوضَع جانبًا ليبرد. تُقطَّع عجينة الكبّة الى كرات متساوية، صغيرة أو متوسطة، وتُعبَّأ بالحشوة وتُشكَّل على شكل بيضوي.

### التغليف

تُخلَط التامبورا مع نصف كوب من الماء البارد في وعاء واحد، وفي وعاء آخر يُوضع فتات الخبز. تُغمس أقراص الكبة في خليط التامبورا ثمّ في فتات الخبز، وتُوضَع قبل القلي في الفريزر لنصف ساعة حتى تتماسك. تُقلى الكبة في زيت عميق وساخن لمدة 3-4 دقائق حتى تصبح ذهبية اللون، ثم تُصفّى وتُوضَع فوق ورق المطبخ لامتصاص الزيت. تُقدَّم الكبة ساخنة بجانب السلطة.

## المقادير

(لـ 10-15 قرصًا)

### عجينة الكبة

3 حبة بطاطا كبيرة الحجم
1 كوب برغل
1 ملعقة كبيرة زيت
1 ملعقة صغيرة ببريكا حلوة
ملح وفلفل أسود حسب الرغبة
½ ملعقة صغيرة كركم

### الحشوة

1 بصلة متوسطة مفرومة
1 ملعقة كبيرة زيت نباتي للقلي
250 غرام فطر شامبينيون مفروم ناعم جدا
¼ كوب صنوبر محمّص
1 ملعقة صغيرة من البهارات التالية: قرفة مطحونة، كمون، بودرة الثوم
ملح وفلفل أسود حسب الرغبة

### للتغليف الكبة

½ كوب خليط التامبورا
فتات الخبز
زيت للقلي

# KNAFEH | الكنافة

"Vegan knafeh? How are you planning to veganize a cheese-based dish?" they asked me at home. Well, not just 'they' – I asked myself as well, realizing this is an advanced vegan challenge. After a couple of imperfect attempts, I decided to use semolina dough, which is more pliable and easier to work with than kadaif noodles. And while we're experimenting with non-traditional knafeh, why not make it cupcake-shaped?

# INGREDIENTS

(Serves 6)

### SEMOLINA DOUGH

2 cups fine semolina
1 cup coconut oil
1 teaspoon natural orange food coloring
  (or ½ teaspoon sweet paprika)

### CHEESE

2 cups non-dairy milk
  (preferably unsweetened almond)
¼ cup vegan butter
¼ cup sugar
1 tablespoon cornstarch
1 cup raw almonds or cashews,
  soaked overnight
1 teaspoon lemon juice
1 teaspoon vanilla extract

### QATAR SYRUP

2 cups brown sugar
1 cup water
1 cup lemon juice
1 cup rosewater

### GARNISH SYRUP

½ cup crushed pistachio

# PREPARATION

### FOR THE SEMOLINA DOUGH

Preheat the oven to 180 degrees C (350 degrees F). In a bowl, mix the semolina with the coconut oil until uniform (it may take about 15 minutes). Add the food coloring or paprika (it won't affect the flavor) and mix well until the dough is evenly colored.

### FOR THE CHEESE

In a pot, heat the milk, butter and sugar. Keep stirring until dissolved.
In a different cup, dissolve the cornstarch in ¼ cup cold water and add to the pot. Cook over low heat for 30 minutes, stirring constantly.
Move the mixture to a food processor, add the almonds (or cashews), lemon and vanilla extract, and blend until smooth.

### FOR THE QATAR SYRUP

Cook the sugar and the water over a medium heat until it dissolves. Add the lemon and rose water and continue stirring until boiling. Lower the heat and cook for 15 more minutes.

### TO ASSEMBLE THE KNAFEH

Grease personal cupcake dishes, fill halfway with dough and press well. Pour the cheese mixture on top. Bake for 20-30 minutes, until the cheese hardens. Let the pastries cool. Carefully turn over onto a serving dish, pour the qatar syrup over each one and sprinkle with crushed pistachios.

## طريقة التحضير

### عجينة السميد

يُخلَط السميد مع زيت جوز الهند في وعاء لمدة ربع ساعة حتى الحصول على قوام متجانس. يُضاف الملوّن الغذائي أو الببريكا (لا تؤثر على الطعم) ويُخلَط حتى يتجانس اللون.

### الجبنة

يُسخّن الحليب في قدر، مع زيت جوز الهند والسكر، مع الاستمرار بالتحريك حتى يذوب المزيج كليًا.

يُذوّب النشاء على حدة في ربع كوب من الماء البارد، ثم يُضاف إلى القدر. يُترك المزيج على نار هادئة لنصف ساعة مع الاستمرار بالتحريك. بعدها يُسكَب في الخلاط الكهربائي ويُطحَن بإضافة اللوز أو الكاجو، ويُضاف إليه عصير الليمون وماء الزهر والفانيليا السائلة حتى الحصول على قوام متجانس.

### القطر

يُذوّب السكر مع الماء في قدر على نار متوسطة حتى يغلي، تُخفَّف الحرارة ويُترك القطر لمدة ربع ساعة إضافية حتى يصبح كثيفًا.

### إعداد الكنافة

تُدهَن قوالب "الكاب-كيك" الشخصية، وتُوضَع فيها عجينة السميد حتى نصف القالب ويُضغط عليها جيّدًا، ثم يُضاف مزيج الحليب، وتُخبز في فرن مسخّن مسبقًا على حرارة 180 درجة لمدة 30-20 دقيقة حتى تتماسك الجبنة. تُترَك القوالب جانبًا حتى تبرد، ثم تُقلَب في طبق تقديم بحذر، ويُسكَب عليها القطر الساخن ويُنثَر فوقها الفستق الحلبي وتُقدَّم ساخنة.

## المقادير

(لِ 6 وجبات)

### لعجينة السميد

2 كوب سميد ناعم

1 كوب زيت جوز الهند

¼ ملعقة ملوّن غذائي برتقالي
(أو ملعقة صغيرة من الببريكا الحلوة)

### للجبنة

2 كوب حليب نباتي
(مفضل حليب لوز غير محلّى)

¼ كوب زيت جوز الهند

¼ كوب سكر (يمكن استبداله بمحلّي آخر)

1 ملعقة كبيرة نشاء

1 كوب لوز أو كاجو نيء منقوع لمدة ليلة كاملة

1 ملعقة صغيرة عصير ليمون

1 ملعقة صغيرة فانيليا سائلة

### للقطر

2 كوب سكر بني

1 كوب ماء

1 ملعقة كبيرة عصير ليمون

1 ملعقة كبيرة ماء زهر

### للتقديم

½ كوب فستق حلبي مطحون

# SEITAN WHEAT PROTEIN | السايتان - بروتين القمح

Gluten (wheat protein) powder can be bought in baking supply stores or modern spice stores. Once you've found it, it's very quick and easy to prepare seitan at home without any special equipment. This short method also allows you to add any desired flavor to the seitan itself, not only to the stock.

# INGREDIENTS

(Makes 6 slices [300 g, 10½ oz])

3 dried shiitake mushrooms,
   without the stem
1 cup gluten powder
¾ cup water

STOCK

1 l water/vegetable stock
¼ cup soy sauce
1 celery stalk, with the leaves
1 bay leaf or couple of parsley stalks,
   with the leaves

# المقادير

(6 شرائح – 300 غرام تقريبًا)

3 حبات فطر شيتاكي جاف (دون الساق)
1 كوب مسحوق بروتين القمح الجاهز
(جلوتين)
¾ كوب ماء

للمرق

1 لتر ماء / مرق خضار
¼ كوب صلصة الصويا
1 ساق كرفس، مع الأوراق
1 ورق غار / بضعة سيقان بقدونس
مع الأوراق

# PREPARATION

Grind the mushrooms into powder. In a bowl, combine them with the gluten. Add water to create a springy dough. Knead well by hand for five minutes, or in a food processor for about 30 seconds. Let rest for 20 minutes.
Boil water with the soy sauce, celery stalk and bay leaf. Shape the dough into an elongated loaf. Cut into 6 even slices, and simmer in the stock for about an hour. I recommend turning the slices over once or twice during that time
Cool in the cooking liquids. If you're not planning to use the seitan immediately, cover it in shrink wrap and freeze it for up to 3 months.

# طريقة التحضير

يُطحَن الفطر حتى يصبح دقيقًا ويُخلَط مع مسحوق بروتين القمح (الجلوتين). يُضاف الماء حتى تتكوّن عجينة ليّنة. نستمر بالعجن لمدة خمس دقائق، أو في الخلّاط الكهربائي لمدة حوالي 30 ثانية، ثم تُترَك العجينة جانبًا لمدة 20 دقيقة.
في هذه الأثناء يُغلى الماء أو مرق الخضار مع صلصة الصويا والكرفس والغار. تُشكَّل العجينة بالطول أو بشكل دائري، وتُقطَّع إلى ست قطع، ثم تطبخ في المرق لمدة ساعة تقريبًا، على نار متوسّطة، مع مراعاة قلب القطع مرة أو مرتين خلال العملية. تُترَك القطع في سائل الطبخ حتى تبرد. إذا لم تستعمل فورًا، يوصى بتغليفها بالنايلون اللاصق وحفظها في الفريزر لمدة لا تزيد عن ثلاثة أشهر.

---

*Recipe courtesy of Gali Lupo Altaratz, from her book The Israeli Vegan Cookbook.

*الوصفة أُخذت من كتاب " طبخ إسرائيلي خُضري" لجالي لوبو الطرتس، من دار النشرزرش.

# HOMEMADE SEITAN | السايتان من الطحين

Kneading the flour and washing the starch away from the protein may seem a Sisyphean task, but I think this is the better method: it's more natural and doesn't require any special ingredients. Also, I think both the flavor and texture of the result is better.

# INGREDIENTS

(Makes 6 slices [300 g, 10½ oz])

3 cups whole wheat flour
3 cups white flour
1½ cups water
Salt

STOCK

1 l water/vegetable stock
¼ cup soy sauce
1 celery stalk, with the leaves
1 bay leaf or couple of parsley stalks,
    with the leaves

# PREPARATION

Using a mixer and a dough hook, combine the salt and flour with enough water to make a hard dough. Knead for 2-3 minutes (you can also knead by hand). Cover the bowl and let rest for 2 hours. Move the bowl to the sink and change the water. Knead the dough inside the water, wash and strain. Repeat the process until all the starch has been washed away and the water stays clear. You should be left with a smaller, very elastic ball. The whole process takes about 15 minutes.
Let the seitan rest for 15 minutes, and prepare the stock as above. Cut the seitan into 6 equal slices and cook in the stock for an hour. Keep the pot covered while cooking.
Cool and store for up to 24 hours in the refrigerator. If you're not planning on using it immediately, lightly squeeze the water out of the seitan and keep in the freezer for up to 3 months.

المقادير

(6 شرائح – 300 غرام تقريبًا)

3 كوب طحين كامل
3 كوب طحين أبيض
1½ كوب ماء
ملح حسب الرغبة

للمرق

1 لتر ماء / مرق خضار
¼ كوب صلصة الصويا
1 ساق كرفس، مع الأوراق
1 ورق غار / بضعة سيقان بقدونس
مع الأوراق

طريقة التحضير

يُوضع الطحين والملح في الخلاط الكهربائي مع أداة العجن. يُضاف القليل من الماء لتشكيل عجينة جامدة. نواصل العجن لمدة 2-3 دقائق. بالإمكان العجن بواسطة اليدين. تُغمَر العجينة بالماء في وعاء الخلط، وتُترك لمدة ساعتين.
يُنقَل الوعاء لحوض الجلي ويتم تبديل الماء، ثم تُعجن العجينة بالماء وتُغسَل وتُصفّى. يتم تكرار العملية حتى يتم التخلّص من النشاء – أي حتى يصبح الماء صافيًا – ويصغر حجم العجينة، وتصبح مرنة ومطاطية جدًّا. تستغرق هذه العملية ربع ساعة تقريبًا. في هذه الأثناء نقوم بإعداد المرق حسب الوصفة أعلاه. يُقطّع السايتان إلى ست شرائح ويُوضَع في المرق لمدة ساعة في قدر مغطّاة. بعد أن يُوضَع جانبًا ليبرد، يُدخَل للثلاجة لمدة 24 ساعة. إذا لم تُستخدم العجينة فورًا، يوصى بعصر السايتان قليلاً وحفظه في الفريز لمدة لا تزيد على ثلاثة أشهر.

---

*Recipe courtesy of Gali Lupo Altaratz, from her book The Israeli Vegan Cookbook.
*الوصفة أُخذت من كتاب " طبخ إسرائيلي خُضري" لجالي لوبو الطرتس، من دار النشر زرش.

# VEGAN MINCE | بروتين الصويا

It's easy, cheap, accessible and healthy to prepare vegan mince yourself. You don't have to use homemade seitan, but I recommend that you do. Vegan mince is an excellent substitute for minced meat in any recipe, except for meatballs.

## INGREDIENTS

(Makes 5 cups)

1½ cup small soy flakes
300 g (10½ oz) seitan
2 large onions
2 tablespoon olive oil
3-5 tablespoon soy sauce

## PREPARATION

Put the soy flakes in a bowl. Cover with water and let soak for 13 minutes. Strain and squeeze well. Using a food processor, chop the seitan into small crumbs.
Chop the onion and fry in olive oil until golden. Add the soy flakes and seitan crumbs.
Gradually add the soy sauce, until the mixture is completely brown. Fry over medium heat for 10 minutes, stirring continuously.
Divide into small portions (1-1½ cups each) and keep frozen.

## المقادير

(ل 5 أكواب)

1½ كوب قطع الصويا المجروش
300 غرام بروتين القمح
2 بصلة كبيرة
2 ملعقة كبيرة زيت زيتون
5-3 ملعقة كبيرة صلصة الصويا

## طريقة التحضير

تُوضع قطع الصويا المجروش في وعاء، وتُغمَر بالماء وتُنقَع لمدة 15 دقيقة، ثمّ تُصفَّى وتُعصَر جيّدًا. يُفرَم بروتين القمح إلى فتات في الخلاط الكهربائي. يُفرَم البصل فرمًا ناعمًا ويُقلَى بزيت الزيتون حتى يصبح لونه ذهبيًّا، ثم تُضاف إليه قطع الصويا المجروش وفتات بروتين القمح. تُضاف صلصة الصويا بالتدريج حتى يصبح الخليط داكن اللون، ثم يُقلَى على نار متوسّطة لمدة عشر دقائق، مع التحريك المستمر. يُقسَّم الخليط إلى وجبات (كوب أو كوب ونصف) ويُحفَظ في الفريزر.

---

*Recipe courtesy of Gali Lupo Altaratz, from her book The Israeli Vegan Cookbook.

*الوصفة أُخذت من كتاب " طبخ إسرائيلي خُضري" لجالي لوبو الطرتس، من دار النشر زرش.

# BASIC VEGETABLE STOCK | مرق الخضار

Use vegetable stock to prepare soups, sauces, stuffed vegetables, stews, casseroles and grains such as couscous, risotto, quinoa and pilaf. You can make a fresh batch every week and freeze it for use as needed. This is the classic recipe, but you can add vegetables, herbs and spices according to your own taste.

# INGREDIENTS

المقادير

(Makes 2 liters [8-8½ cups])

1 celery root
1 parsley root
3 carrots
1 large onion
5 celery stalks, with the leaves
3 garlic cloves, whole
1 bunch fresh parsley
2 liters water
1 tablespoon salt

1 جذر كرفس
1 جذر بقدونس
3 حبة جزر
1 بصلة كبيرة
5 سيقان كرفس مع الأوراق
3 فصوص ثوم
حزمة بقدونس طازج
2 لتر ماء
1ملعقة كبيرة ملح

# PREPARATION

طريقة التحضير

Wash the vegetables well and peel the roots. In a pot, arrange the roots whole with the celery and parsley stalks over them. Cover with 2 liters of water, add the salt and bring to a boil. Cook over low heat for an hour. Strain the stock to remove the vegetables (you can use them in other dishes) and keep the liquid.

تُغسَل الخضار جيّدًا، وتُقشَّر الجذور. تُوضَع جميع المكوّنات كما هي في قدر مع 2 لتر ماء والملح وتُغطّى حتى تغلي، ثم تُخفَّف الحرارة وتُترَك على نار هادئة لمدة ساعة.
يُصفّى المرق ويُحفَظ للاستعمالات المختلفة. يمكن استعمال الخضار المسلوقة في وصفات أخرى.

نصيحة

**TIP**

If you're in a hurry and need vegetable stock for a certain recipe, you can substitute two tablespoons of instant soup dissolved in water for 3 cups of stock. Fresh, homemade stock is, of course, always better.

من المفضل طبعًا استعمال المرق الطازج، ولكن إذا لم يتّسع الوقت لتحضيره، فيمكن الاستعاضة عنه بإذابة ملعقتين كبيرتين من مسحوق الحساء الخضري في 3 أكواب من الماء.

# VEGAN YOGHURT | اللبن النباتي

Yoghurt is an essential ingredient in the Arab cuisine, and the basis for a wide array of dishes in this book, from main courses to desserts. And what's better than homemade yoghurt? After consulting experienced vegan cooks and experimenting in my own kitchen, I found what I feel to be the winning recipe. To successfully prepare your own yoghurt – follow the instructions carefully and make sure to keep as sanitary as possible.

## INGREDIENTS

(Makes 1 liter [1 quart])

1 liter (1 quart) unsweetened soy milk
5 vegan probiotic capsules
    (available in pharmacies)

## PREPARATION

Heat the soy milk to exactly 45 degrees C (113 degrees F) – use a kitchen thermometer and be careful not to overheat. Move to a sterilized glass jar. Empty the probiotic capsules into the jar – only the powder, without the shell. Mix with a sterilized spoon (boil the spoon in water to sterilize it).
Seal the jar and keep somewhere shaded (but not refrigerated) until the yoghurt thickens. It should take between 12 hours and a day, depending on the ambient temperature.
**How do you know the yoghurt is ready?** After 12 hours shake the jar and watch to see if the liquid has thickened. If it did, refrigerate it for at least 2 hours. If not, wait up to 12 more hours before refrigerating.

WORKING PROCEDURES

• Have a kitchen thermometer ready in advance to measure the milk's temperature precisely.
• Be careful to keep the preparation process sterile and hygienic so as not to introduce unwanted bacteria into the yoghurt. Boiling the jar and spoon and not touching the yoghurt directly will help the success of the process.

WORKING PROCEDURES

• You can keep one cup of the finished yoghurt to use as a base for the next batch, instead of probiotic capsules.
• The yoghurt can be used as an ingredient in the various recipes in the book, and can also be eaten as is.
• To prepare sweet yoghurt, you can use date honey, or other sweeteners, and add your favorite fruit. To prepare a tart yoghurt, you can add salt, lemon, spices and herbs, according to taste.

# المقادير

1 لتر حليب صويا غير محلّى
5 كبسولات البروبيوتيك
(متوقّرة في الصيدليات، ويفضّل النوع
الذي يحتوي على كمية كبيرة ومتنوعة
من البكتيريا)

# طريقة التحضير

يُسخَّن حليب الصويا لدرجة 45 مئوية بالضبط لا أكثر (تُقاس درجة الحرارة بميزان خاص)، ثم يُسكَب في وعاء زجاجي مُعقّم (أي مغسول بالماء المغلي). تُضاف المادة التي في الكبسولات (دون غلاف الكبسولة) إلى الوعاء، ويُحرّك المزيج بملعقة معقّمة.

يُغلَق الوعاء الزجاجي جيّدًا ويُغطَّى بقطعة قماش نظيفة، ويوضَع في الظلّ (ليس في الثلاجة) حتى يجمد الحليب ويتحوّل إلى لبن. تحتاج هذه العملية إلى مدة تتراوح بين 12 ساعة حتى 24 ساعة، حسب درجة حرارة المكان.

**كيف نعرف أن اللبن جاهز؟** بعد مرور 12 ساعة نخضّ الوعاء لنفحص مدى تماسك السائل. إن لم يكن متماسكًا علينا الانتظار لمدة 12 ساعة أخرى، وإن كان متماسكًا نضعه في الثلاجة لمدة ساعتين على الأقل.

• من المستحسن حيازة ميزان حرارة للطبخ، لفحص درجة حرارة الحليب المضبوطة.
• من المهم جدًا المحافظة على نظافة الأدوات (بالذات الوعاء الزجاجي وملعقة التحريك) وتعقيمها، كيلا تدخل إلى اللبن بكتيريا غير مرغوب بها. من المهم أيضًا عدم إدخال اليد في اللبن.

• يمكن حفظ كوب من اللبن واستعماله للترويب مرة أخرى بدلا من كبسولات البروبيوتيك.
• اللبن ملائم للاستعمال كمكوّن في وصفات أخرى من الكتاب، ويمكن أيضًا تناوله باردًا غير مطبوخ.
• لتحضير اللبن الحلو يمكن تحليته بالسيلان (مربّى التمر) أو بمحلّي آخر وإضافة الفواكه حسب الرغبة.
• لتحضير اللبن الحامض يمكن إضافة الملح وعصير الليمون والبهارات والأعشاب الجافة حسب الرغبة.

# DIETARY ADVICE Nataly Shvinkelstain

STEWED TOMATO OKRA Okra contains substances called mucilages, which are very good for the digestive system and restore mucous membranes. Okra is, therefore, very effective at detoxification and regulating bowel movements. Okra is rich in folic acid, magnesium, calcium, vitamin A and B-group vitamins.

STUFFED VINE LEAVES Vine leaves are rich in calcium, zinc, magnesium, iron, B-group vitamins (especially folic acid), vitamin A and essential fatty acids, such as omega-3. Try and find fresh leaves rather than preserved, which may contain artificial preservatives and added salt.

HOMEMADE HUMMUS Replacing regular tahini with whole, sprouted sesame tahini will greatly increase the mineral content and health benefits of your hummus. For example, white, hulled sesame tahini contains about 100 mg calcium per 100 g, while whole sesame tahini has almost 1000 mg per 100 g. The difference is significant in other minerals as well. Sprouting the sesame helps to break down the acids inside (such as phytic acid and oxalic acid), and by extension, the body's mineral absorption. In addition, whole sesame tahini is usually cold pressed while regular tahini usually uses roasted sesame seeds.

MA'AMOUL Coconut oil is very healthy. It contains essential fatty acids and is stable at high temperatures, relative to other oils. Be aware, though, that it has a dominant flavor, making it less suitable for people who don't like its taste.

STUFFED CABBAGE Cabbage is very good for the digestive system, acts as an anti-inflammatory, and soothes ulcers. It restores mucous membranes in the bowels and helps prevent colon cancer. It contains powerful anti-oxidants as well as, calcium, potassium, magnesium, iron, some vitamin E and some B-group vitamins, among others.

RICE WITH LENTILS AND RADISH SALAD Combining grains (such as rice) with legumes (such as lentils) in the same dish provides all of the amino acids needed for a balanced, complete protein. You can substitute whole basmati rice for the white rice for an appreciable addition of vitamins and nutritional fibers, which are important to regulate bowel function and blood fat levels, affecting heart health. Lentils are rich in folic acid and B-group vitamins. They are also rich in iron, zinc, potassium, calcium and magnesium.

LOUBIEH AND COUSCOUS Like all legumes, black-eyed peas are high in fiber, protein and many vitamins. They are nutritious, aid in regulating blood sugar levels and contribute to a healthy heart and digestive system. Pairing them with couscous, which is a wheat product, makes the dish a complete protein source. Whole wheat couscous is preferable, as it adds fiber and vitamins to the dish.

COLORFUL STUFFED VEGETABLE CASSEROLE Rich in pigments, peppers are an excellent source of anti-oxidants. The colors yellow, orange, red and green indicate anti-oxidants, which help the body fight free radicals, and so aid in preventing and even treating various illnesses. In addition, peppers are rich in vitamin C, which boosts the immune system.

MALUKHIYAH STEW WITH BLACK QUINOA Malukhiyah is made of the young, green leaves of the bush okra plant. The leaves are rich in protein, calcium, iron, potassium, B-group vitamins and vitamin C, as well as chlorophyll, which helps detoxify the body.

TURKISH DUMPLINGS For a healthy upgrade, use mushrooms, chopped and sautéed with onion in extra-virgin cold pressed olive oil instead of vegan mince. You can also replace half of the flour with whole spelt flour for more dietary fiber, vitamins and minerals.

RA'IF WITH VEGAN MINCE Instead of vegan mince, try thin slices of organic tofu. Tofu is rich in high quality protein, calcium, iron, magnesium and other minerals. When fried on a pan with the right seasoning, tofu has a meat-like texture, and a gives a tasty and filling end result.

EGGPLANT-TAHINI SPREAD Eggplant is an excellent source of B-group vitamins, dietary fibers, potassium and magnesium and also contains zinc and calcium. Eggplants contain important anti-oxidants such as anthocyanin which protect against free radicals. Regular consumption of eggplants can help slow aging processes and prevent diseases.

RICE AND VEGGIE UPSIDE DOWN CAKE Health upgrade ideas:
* Add ¼ cup cooked chickpeas, for complete protein.
* Substitute whole basmati rice for the white rice, to add dietary fiber and vitamins.
* Garnish the dish with fresh chopped herbs: dill, coriander, parsley, etc.

FALAFEL Health upgrade ideas:
* Bake the falafel balls instead of frying. You can brush them with a little olive oil.
* Use whole wheat or whole spelt breadcrumbs.
* Fry in a little grapeseed oil, rather than deep-frying.
* Use spelt flour or whole wheat pitas for complete protein and added dietary fiber and vitamins.
* Eat the falafel with a plate of hummus and whole, sprouted sesame tahini.

WHITE BEANS AND QUINOA Quinoa, while not technically a grain, is considered the mother of all grains. It contains all essential amino acids, and is therefore a source of complete protein. Quinoa is rich in iron, calcium, magnesium and many vitamins, as well as dietary fibers which aid in regulating blood fat levels and bowel movements.

BASBUSE You can use whole wheat semolina, to give the cake higher nutritional value. Whole semolina contains the husk, where most of the vitamins and mineral are.

POTATO KUBEH Potatoes are used in a variety of unhealthy foods, which is why they have the reputation of being unhealthy. But in fact, they are very nutritious. Potatoes are rich in B-group vitamins and contain iron, calcium, zinc and magnesium. In addition, potatoes are high in dietary fiber, which help keep you full. Try to eat them unpeeled when possible – the fibers in the skin aid in regulating sugar absorption.

MUSHROOM PASTRIES Nutritional yeast is deactivated yeast, rich in B-group vitamins, iron, zinc and potassium, you can replace half of the flour with whole spelt flour – spelt is tasty and easy to digest, and can upgrade this dish by adding nutritious fiber and vitamins.

TRIANGLE SPINACH PASTRIES Spinach, like all greens, is rich in vitamins and minerals. Spinach leaves are high in folic acid, vitamin A, calcium, magnesium and iron and retain their nutritional value when cooked.
Replacing half of the white flour with whole wheat or spelt flour will add more vitamins, minerals and dietary fiber, as well as satisfy hunger and regulate blood sugar levels.

'GOULASH' WITH PEAS AND SOY CHUNKS Soy contains complete proteins with all essential amino acids. I recommend buying organic soy flakes or organic tofu, to avoid genetically modified products.

POTATOES STUFFED WITH RED RICE Red rice is a whole grain. The red pigment, antocyanin, protects against disease and aging processes. Red rice is rich in fiber and many vitamins.

FAVA BEAN AND HERB DIP Fava beans are rich in protein and very filling, thanks to their high fiber content. They also contain vitamin A, B-group vitamins, magnesium, iron and minerals.

SEITAN EGGROLL Seitan is made of gluten, wheat protein. It has a texture resembling meat, and is a good culinary substitute. In terms of health it adds protein to the menu, but is not suitable for people with celiac disease or gluten sensitivity.

JAM COOKIES Oats are a particularly nutritious grain, suitable for every age and almost every individual. Oats are rich in protein, fiber, iron, calcium, potassium, magnesium and B-group vitamins.

TABULE SALAD Bulgur is wheat that has been cooked, dried and ground into varying level of thickness (coarse or fine). Bulgur is fast to prepare because it is already cooked, and still contains various health advantages such as fiber and minerals. Bulgur is not suitable for people suffering from gluten sensitivity and can be replaced with quinoa, buckwheat or millet, which do not contain gluten and can serve as a variation on a familiar dish.

PITA WITH ZA'ATAR AND LABANE Za'atar is the name of a spice mix containing mostly Syrian oregano (Origanum syriacum). In addition to its familiar, popular flavor, it has certain curative properties, and is especially effective in strengthening the immune system and supporting the digestive system.

SINYET AL-KUFTA Red lentils are easy to digest and contain a lot of protein. All lentils contain B-group vitamins, iron, calcium and potassium, and are also rich in fiber, which assists in bowel function and regulating blood fat and sugar levels.

'IJET AL-BROCCOLI Broccoli, the king of vegetables, contains many vitamins and minerals: vitamin A, vitamin C, B-group vitamins including folic acid, vitamin K, vitamin E, potassium, calcium, magnesium, iron and more. In addition, broccoli contains dietary fiber which aids bowel function and promotes intestinal flora.

FATTOUSH A wonderful example of a 5-color salad. Eating vegetables is very important to our health and has been proven to prevent disease. Vegetables are rich in vitamins and minerals that are essential to the proper functioning of our organs and bodily systems. Each color offers different health benefits. Vegetables are low in fat and calories. They have a high dietary fiber content, which means they help stave off hunger.

CAULIFLOWER AND MILLET Millet is a common name for a number of different grains, all rich in iron, calcium, magnesium, B-group vitamins, protein and dietary fibers. Millet does not contain gluten and is therefore suitable for people with celiac disease.

SEITAN AND MUSHROOM SHAWARMA There are many varieties of mushrooms. They boost the immune system and raise energy levels. Not all mushrooms are edible, but the ones that are usually contain B-group vitamins including folic acid, selenium, potassium, iron, phosphorus, zinc, magnesium and some vitamin D (mushrooms should not be relied on as a sole source for vitamin D, however).

DUMPLINGS IN YOGHURT SAUCE Replacing half of the flour with whole wheat or whole spelt flour would give this dish a health upgrade and add vitamins, minerals and dietary fiber. In addition, you can bake the dumplings instead of frying.

SHAKSHUKA Although regarded as a vegetable, botanically the tomato is a fruit. It contains carotenoids, a group of pigments (red, orange and yellow) which are important to the eyes, the skin, the digestive system and the immune system. Alongside other vitamins and minerals, tomatoes also contain the anti-oxidant lycopene, which is considered especially effective in preventing diseases, particularly cancer.

# ACKNOWLEDGMENTS

First, I wish I could hug each and every individual, each heart that has beaten for this project. I dedicate this book to everyone who gave of their time and effort so it could become a reality. To everyone who shared, wrote about, and supported it.

A huge thanks to my 1,102 Headstart supporters. If I could, I'd have written all of your names here. Thanks to you, my dream became our dream, which then became our book. Everyone whose heart is hungry for change – whether they are vegans who want a more compassionate world, humans who want to see the end of war, or people who like to cook – each has breathed life into this project with their own unique perspective.

Many thanks to Zeresh Books, to Dr. Thamar Eilam Gindin and Yuval Kaplan, who gave me round-the-clock support, streamlining the crowdfunding process and saving me from a lot of mistakes. They were by my side through the entire process and they still are, picking up whatever I drop. They're exactly the kind of people who make this world a more beautiful place.

A special thanks to the author Joei Avniel, who gave me the inspiration for the book and the courage to launch a crowdfunding campaign.
Many great thanks to all the reporters and radio hosts who invited me for interviews and publicized my idea in the media: Radio two's Eran Singer, Radio Kol Israel in Arabic's Yazid Khadid, Local Talk's Lilach Ben-David, Yedioth Aharonoth and YNET's Yehuda Shochat, MAKO's Rita Goldstein, MyNET's Yifat Burshtein and Hamakor's (Almasdar) Hadas Harosh.

Thank you to my test cooks , who tried the recipes and gave me thorough and accurate critiques: Meitar Goldin, Neta Rozner-Goldfeiz, Ahd Dasuki, Amira Dasuka, Anat Zamberg, Anastasia Hatib, Aviv Zakai, Amit Moravtzik, Ester kremer, Sofia Navarro, Ayah Awad, Merav Shochat-Khalamish, Dikla Rom, Shirly Shefer, RUTH MASHAT, Jawan Kharboush, Dr. Muzna Bshara, Nitzan harel, Tamar Landau, Ortal Sarur, Ronit Tur, Or Koren, Misa Faour, Israel Greenheuz, Lilach and Ella Baumer, Ayelet Rotman, Rania Tchan-Saba, Reuven Kaplan, orit tsabari-elmaliach, Meydad Feldman, Nitzan Shaul, Mana Feiner, Bar Tauber, Yuval Kaplan, Julian Ibrahim, Nehorai Saban.

A special thanks to Hemdat Gavriely for the daily support throughout the publishing process, for her preliminary edits to the introduction, for all the tips and encouragement, and mainly for her faith in the success of the crowdfunding campaign.
A special thanks to everyone who worked on the book, and maintained the highest possible quality in every area.

Thank you to the Vegan Cooking facebook group for advertising the project to vegans and for their substitution suggestions, and especially to Guy Mughrabi, one of the group's admins.

Thank you to Chen Elbilia and Chen Brailowsky for suggesting the english title.

A big thank you to my dear family and friends who stood by me all along the way and fed me with a lot of love and good energy so I could carry on.

# SPONSORSHIPS

**Nataly Shvinkelstain** is a naturopath (N.D), a graduate of Ridman college of alternative medicine, a mother of vegan-since-birth children, and the author of the best-selling *The secret of the vegan baby's diet*, a guide to raising vegan babies. The book includes 80 diverse recipes and guidance according to age. It's been published in Israel and abroad. Nataly guides families in developing personalized vegan, balanced diets. She works with individuals and groups. Nataly has extensive experience in using vegan diets to treat and manage a variety of diseases that conventional medicine labels chronic. In addition, she has developed her own brand of healing herb formulas, Nataly's Formulas, which she markets in natural shops.

Since 2007 she has had a vegan recipe blog "Healthy Recipes Photographed" – one of the first of its kind on the Israeli internet. She also admins a facebook group called "Veganism and health" which hosts thousands of members. There she answers questions regarding health issues.

Since 2006 she manages a large internet site which includes information regarding: diseases, healing herbs, traditional medicine, vitamins, minerals, veganism and naturopathic medicine, and more.

Nataly Shvinkelstain's clinic is in Holon. Operating hours can be found on her website.

www.to-heal.com
nataly210@gmail.com
+972-54-2037734

---

**Darma** – the place for yoga in Rehovot, offers a variety of yoga classes suited for everyone: Yoga of various styles and levels for younger and older practitioners, pre-natal yoga, children and teen yoga, baby yoga, and more.

At Darma we take yoga seriously and offer you the best teachers in the area at our spacious studio, especialy built and equipped for the practice of yoga.

Darma supports eco-friendly living, veganism, equality and tolerance.

www.darmayoga.co.il
+972-8-942073

**Veganz ltd** is a young family company. We've made it our business to bring to Israel the richness of the greater vegan culinary world. Our products are exclusively vegan and exclusively delicious. Our goal is to expand the food options for Israel's vegans. We develop, produce, import, and export healthy vegan substitutes across a range of food groups, and we're working to develop many new products to enlarge the typical daily vegan menu. Our products are all plant-based, and answer to a vegan's unique dietary needs. Veganz products have the "vegan friendly" stamp and are available in natural shops throughout Israel.

www.veganz.co.il

---

**Best Vegan Dishes** is a site that supports the home-cooking and other needs of vegans around the world, is happy to take part in publishing this important and tasty new book. Congratulations to Kifah Dasuki!

Cooking and eating vegan food can be a challenge – striking the balance between the limited ingredients and the human desire to create delightful dishes. Kifah gives us an opportunity to acquaint ourselves with traditional dishes and revamp our recipe collection. There's nothing like good food to open hearts and bring people together. May this book inspire readers in the kitchen and nurture communities.

We know that another challenge for vegans can be finding restaurants while travelling on vacation or for business. That is why we founded Best Vegan Dishes, where you can find:
* Recommendations for vegan friendly restaurants
* Vegan recipes from across the internet
* Ideas for vegan meals for kids
* And more

 You're always welcome to visit us:
www.bestvegandishes.com

# A-B TABLE OF CONTENTS | الفهرس

I really want to thank you for reading my book. I sincerely hope that you received value from it and enjoy it

This book is my dream and it's about making a difference!  it's my pleasure that you are a part of it

If you received value from this book, then I would  like to ask you for a favor. Would you be kind  enough to leave a review for this book on Amazon? Scan QR

37906466R00095

Made in the USA
Middletown, DE
03 March 2019